REVISED AND UPDATED

WRITE TO THE TOP

Writing for Corporate Success

REVISED AND UPDATED

WRITE TO THE TOP

Writing for Corporate Success

DEBORAH DUMAINE

RANDOM HOUSE
New York

Grateful acknowledgment is made to Howard W. Sams & Com-
pany for permission to reprint excerpts from *The Macintosh Advisor: Essential Techniques for Experienced Users* by Cynthia Harriman
and Bencion Calica. Copyright © 1986 by Cynthia Harriman
and Bencion Calica. Reproduced with permission of the publisher, Howard W. Sams & Co., Indianapolis.

Library of Congress Cataloging-in-Publication Data

Dumaine, Deborah.
Write to the top.

1. Business writing. 2. English language—Business
English. 3. Business communication—Data processing.
I. Title.
HF5718.3.D85   1989   658.4'53   88-43226
ISBN 0-679-72346-3

Manufactured in the United States of America
35798642

Dedicated with love
to my family

Acknowledgments

This revision of *Write to the Top* reflects not only my ideas, but the insights and originality of the Better Communications trainers. Building on the concepts in the first edition, several of our trainers joined the rewrite effort by contributing new approaches and documenting our latest strategies. This new version sums up our most recent five years of working with corporations and coincides with Better Communications' tenth anniversary.

It's hard to know where to begin thanking people because so many contributed so much. I can't say enough about the enthusiasm and ingenuity of our trainers. Their dedication makes our workshops and the techniques in this book top-notch. My enormous thanks go to the following colleagues:

For brainstorming, writing, and editing new chapters: June August, Diane Kellogg, Stephanie E. Bernstein, Phyllis Meyer, Patricia Hamilton, Barbara Blanchard, Larry Raskin, and Deborah Whitehouse.

For help with copy-editing and manuscript preparation: Judith Wolff, Maureen Connaughton, Mary Kennedy, and Liz Stillman.

For their ongoing creative suggestions for improving our workshops: Yvonne Chabrier, Lucie Arbuthnot, Tom Gorman, Dan Schlieben, Jane Evanson, and Jane Shaw.

For good-humoredly keeping the business afloat while I disappeared for a few months: Deborah Daw, Mary Kennedy, Miriam Dumaine, Jessica Forbes, and Chad Rosen.

For her relentless dedication to the excellence of this manuscript, for her encouragement, and patience: Charlotte Mayerson, my Random House editor.

Many people contributed greatly to the original edition of five years ago. My continuing thanks go to Sherri Federbush for her assistance as developmental editor. Others who offered valuable editorial suggestions were: Ann Blum, Priscilla Claman, Brian Dumaine, Lisa Danchi, Eve Goodman, Marea Gordett, Karen Horowitz, Alex Johnson, Carolyn Russell, Harry Saxman, Michael Segal, Caroline Sutton, Jenny Webster, and, above all, my sister Miriam Dumaine.

Contents

Introduction

Since *Write to the Top* was first published, the response from readers and clients has been extremely enthusiastic. It's been gratifying to hear people say that our techniques have saved them time and increased their effectiveness at work. We have updated the book to share with our readers Better Communications' newest strategies and latest breakthroughs. We also wanted to pass along the excitement that comes with mastering one of the hardest parts of most people's jobs.

Good writing is a powerful tool: it can make your message stand out from the mass of material that competes for attention in corporations every day. Good writing focuses your ideas for impact and helps you get the response you want from your colleagues. If you can't write clearly and powerfully, your career advancement will always be seriously limited.

The larger the corporation, the greater the need for concise, clear writing. Executives don't have the time—or the inclination—to unravel poorly organized material. Whether you're writing a letter, a sales memo, or a detailed financial report, it is crucial that you write lucidly and persuasively. Even outstanding ideas can be defeated by mediocre writing.

As a writer, corporate trainer, editor, reading specialist, and former faculty member at Simmons Graduate School of Management, I have spent the last ten years developing writing-improvement techniques specifically designed to meet the needs of corporate writers. My company, Better Communications, has successfully used these methods to develop managers' skills in Fortune 1,000 companies nationwide.

Through workshops and private counseling, my staff and I have taught managers and executives how to achieve a special edge in the competitive world of business by giving their ideas the proper form and expression. We've also assembled techniques and exercises for overcoming writer's block, modernizing style, and increasing writing speed.

Write to the Top is divided into three parts. The first part presents the Six Steps to Reader-Centered Writing. You'll learn how to begin the writing process by analyzing your purpose and your audience (Step 1), then how to generate ideas and get the writing process started (Step 2). Steps 3 and 4 involve grouping information and sequencing your ideas for the best results. Finally, Steps 5 and 6 go into detail about writing, then editing your document.

Part Two, titled *Writing to Influence,* illustrates how to get action from your writing and how to complete writing projects with other people—team writing.

Part Three helps you with more specific problems of grammar and editing. The Better Communications method divides the writing task into a series of subskills. You can pinpoint your individual strengths and weaknesses in each area as you go along and then follow the appropriate exercises, which are, incidentally, fun to do. Some of your skills may only need to be reviewed; others may require more serious attention. The on-site workshop we deliver to corporate clients is self-paced and individualized. The exercises in this book reflect the same approach.

Like most skills, writing is improved primarily by practice. This book offers both guidance and practice exercises to sharpen your writing ability and make this daily task less burdensome. The strategies in this book all work—but only if you do. You must get involved in order to learn. No one becomes a faster jogger simply by reading a book about jogging; neither will you improve your writing by reading a book or listening to a lecture. This book offers a tested program that asks that you *write* as well as read. Just as running laps improves your running, every page you actually work on will benefit your writing.

PART ONE

Six Steps to Reader-Centered Writing

To write simply
is as difficult as to be good.
W. SOMERSET MAUGHAM

Why Write?

Is this you?

Tom LeBlanc glances at his watch and then back to the empty page in front of him. The ticking of the wall clock grows louder, and a siren outside the window makes him lose his train of thought for the second time. The right words are just beyond his reach.

His mind wanders to the next day's appointments and to the movie he is going to see with Elaine that evening. A ringing telephone brings his attention back to the memo he wants to write. He thinks, *I'm just not getting anywhere. I know pretty much what I want to say, but I can't get those first words out. I want to hint to Jack that I know who made the calls to Honolulu during the office party. But how to phrase it in this memo so the whole office doesn't take it as an attack on Jack? I want each person to think the memo applies to everyone equally.*

Tom stands, straightens up his desk, and wonders if a cup of coffee will wake him up. "Maybe I'll just let it go until tomorrow," he mutters.

Most of us resist writing in some way

We have all felt at one time or another the way this manager does. Whether writing a long report or a short memo, we find ourselves staring at the blank page or screen more often than we'd care to admit. At those times, the process can seem so overwhelming that we will do anything to avoid putting pen to paper.

We get into this trouble because most of us were not taught an effective step-by-step approach to the writing process. We were often told, with bright red pen, what we were doing wrong, but few teachers ever said, "Write this way!"

Convenient distractions

In the office, there are many distractions: the phone rings, an associate drops by, or there's an easy, mechanical job to do. Here is a list of obstacles to writing mentioned by members of a business-writing workshop I conducted:

- I need to clean my entire office before I can start writing.
- I can't find the time to do my job and write this proposal, too.
- The boss called a special meeting.
- No matter what I write, it will be ripped to shreds.
- I don't understand why Dick wants me to put this in writing.
- I can't write until I've clipped my fingernails.

For those who dread beginning or who are embarrassed about their skills, almost any other activity will win out over writing.

Our mass media society sabotages good writing skills

Telephones and video make it possible to communicate with a minimum of reading or writing. Television connects us with news, entertainment, and information. Telephones transmit messages quickly and easily over great distances. As much as we may long for simpler times, computerized communications and teleconferences are a reality.

As we rely less on letters and literature, we are becoming far less comfortable with the written word, whether on paper or a display screen. People read dramatically fewer books than they did fifty years ago, and it shows.

No wonder many people say that writing is the part of their job they like the least. In fact, most of them would probably be happy to see other methods of communication replace writing completely.

Writing skills will always be vital to business success

Most business people I meet are not happy with their writing skills. On top of this, they are now being asked to write using a computer or to make decisions about graphics such as type styles—tasks that are alien to most. No matter how technological the workplace may become, real power will still have its source in the written word.

Good writing skills are in demand by employers, according to an article about business schools in *Time* magazine. Why? Skill in writing correlates highly with the ability to think well—to analyze information, weigh alternatives, and make decisions.

Another article, in the *Harvard Business Review,* listed writing ability as one of the critical skills possessed by those who reach the top strata of corporations. Our experience consulting with executives verifies that these days no one gets to the top without being able to write well.

The challenge of business writing today

No matter what the topic, most of the writing we, as trainers, see suffers from one major failing: it is written more from the point of view of the writer than from an angle that will appeal to the reader. One of the greatest challenges to writers is to get outside of their personal interests to present their ideas in a way that will answer every reader's four biggest questions:

1. Why should I read this?
2. What's this about?
3. What's in this for me?
4. What am I being asked to do?

We will be explaining more about reader-centered writing and how to achieve it as we go through the Six Steps that follow. You'll see how the *reader-centered* approach will make your writing more influential. It will help you achieve the results you want.

Writing as an aid to decision making

Have you ever noticed how talking to a friend sometimes helps you sort out and make better decisions? During the writing process, you can relate to the paper as you would to a friend to see what you're thinking about and examine the subtleties. Many people keep personal journals just for this reason. Often, writing helps people reach important decisions, whether personal or business. As W. H. Auden said, "How can I know what I think until I see what I say?"

Writing benefits the writer

One manager wrote a long document developing an idea for a new business direction. As he proceeded with the writing, he changed his mind about the value of pursuing the new direction and actually decided to recommend aborting the project. He reported that the writing process helped him see the facts more objectively. He had been so emotionally tied to his great idea that until he put it in writing, he wasn't able to think it through clearly.

Writing is thought on paper: a tool for helping to create and organize ideas. When writers transfer random ideas from the brain to paper, they begin to understand their own thoughts better. As they continue the process and develop a polished document for readers, they refine their ideas.

Writing benefits the reader

Some information is simply too complex for oral communication alone. Without a written document as an aid to memory and understanding, sophisticated information is difficult to absorb and interpret. Readers must also have the option of returning to certain sections to review details.

When is it best to write?

Whatever business you're in, there are countless situations in which a written document is the best approach (see the chapter on Negotiations and Strategies in Part Two). Below are eight objectives that often require a written document. For many of these objectives, writing can be combined with speaking for a stronger result.

1. To influence
2. To make initial sales contacts
3. To recognize achievements
4. To C.Y.A. (cover your anatomy)
5. To announce news, changes and surprises
6. To report results of research
7. To analyze problems
8. To evaluate the performance of people, products, or processes

Other common types of business documents

For those of you who are just starting out in business writing, here's a partial list of the most common types of writing we see in our workshops.

Annual Report	Organizational Memo	Request for Proposal
Apology Letter	Performance Appraisal	(RFP)
Audit Report	Planning Report	Research Report
Decision Needed	Position Paper	Sales-Call Report
Engineering Report	Problem-Solving	Sales Letter
Feasibility Study	Memo	Status Report
Information Request	Procedural Change	Test Protocol
Marketing Letter	Procedure Manual	Training Materials
Meeting	Proposal	Trip Report
Announcement	Recommendation	Work Order
Memo	Report	
Minutes of a Meeting		

So, are you ready to begin?

It's easy to know *why* to write. The challenge is knowing *how* to reach out to your readers and how to write efficiently. We recommend Six Steps to Reader-Centered Writing. It's as easy as 1, 2, 3 . . . 4, 5, 6!

WHY SIX STEPS?

How do efficient writers write? Some seem to have a natural flair, while others develop the skill through practice. Most of the participants in our writing workshops confirm that their writing improves when they begin to look at it as a manageable process, rather than as an irritating chore. How is this shift in attitude possible? By breaking the writing task into its components.

The Six Steps present writing as an easy-to-learn method. Using this systematic approach, you always know where you are in the process. That way, even if you're interrupted, you can pick up where you left off. This is especially important if you're working on more than one document at a time.

Why the emphasis on Reader-Centered Writing?

I've seen writers with superb skill in the techniques of writing get poor or apathetic responses from their readers. Why? They were too caught up in their own agenda to put themselves in their readers' shoes. Perhaps they said too much or too little; but whatever the reason, they lost their audience. One of the biggest complaints we get from readers is, "I don't know what he's driving at in this memo."

The phrase *I understand where you're coming from* became popular in the eighties because communicators of every sophistication level rediscovered that being other-oriented is the key to getting a message across. Many people practice this technique in oral communication, but most lag behind in applying it to the written word.

Here, then, is an outline of the professional business writer's process. The good news: 80% of our workshop graduates report that they have cut their writing time by one third and have achieved enthusiastic reader response to their documents.

THE SIX STEPS TO
READER-CENTERED WRITING

Reader-Centered Writing involves three phases:
planning, drafting, and editing.

Step 1 Analyze your purpose and audience.
    Use the Focus Sheet on page 10.

Step 2 Generate ideas.
    Use one of the Start-up Strategies on pages 14–29.

Step 3 Group information under headlines.
    Organize your ideas with one of our methods of
    development starting on page 30.

Step 4 Sequence your ideas.
    The bottom line should go on top—most of the time.

Step 5 Write the first draft.
    1. Quickly write a paragraph for each headline.
    2. Get distance from your document for a while.

Resist editing until Step 6!

Step 6 Edit for clarity, conciseness, and accuracy.
    1. Use the "Be Your Own Editor" Checklist on pages 65–66.
    2. Use How to Design for Visual Impact on page 69.

Analyze Your Purpose and Audience

When you start a letter or memo, you are starting a relationship: you will need cooperation and agreement from the reader for the relationship to work. It's best to begin by knowing what you want, and by understanding what the other person expects. The more you consider your reader, the better your chances of getting the response you desire.

COMPLETE THE FOCUS SHEET

To start this relationship, create a reader profile. Although you may not know your readers personally, use your experience to answer some basic questions about who they are and what you want to communicate. The following Focus Sheet will help you clarify what you intend to accomplish with your memo, letter, or report, and will keep your writing on target. Use the Focus Sheet to begin every writing project.

How to answer the questions

By answering the questions on the Focus Sheet, you've started planning your document. You are bringing it into focus. Each question on the Focus Sheet is directed at a specific issue you must analyze as you prepare your document. For example:

- "Reader's Role" will determine your tone.
- "Reader's Knowledge" will determine content and vocabulary.
- "Document's Use" will influence your format.

Let's look at each of the four areas in detail.

STEP #1: THE FOCUS SHEET

Answer these questions as the first step in any writing task:

1. **Purpose:**
   - Why am I writing this? _____
   - What do I want the reader to do? _____

2. **Audience:**
   - Who is/are my reader(s)? _____

   - What is the reader's role? _____

   - What does the reader know about the subject? _____

   - How will the reader react? _____

   - What is my reader's style? Should I adjust to it? _____

   - How will the reader use this document? _____

   - Whom should I include in this mailing? _____

3. **Bottom Line:**
   If the reader were to forget everything else, what one key point do I want remembered? _____
   _____
   _____
   _____

4. **Strategy:**
   - Should *I* be writing this? At *this* time?
     Would a phone call or meeting be more effective?

   - Should I send this at all? Am I too late?

   - Is someone else communicating the same information?
     Should I check with that person?

   - Should I include deadlines? Actions requested?

   - Is my method of transmission the best? For example, should I be using electronic mail, traditional mail, or fax?

PURPOSE

What are some of your typical reasons for writing? Here are a few:

to persuade	to analyze	to explain
to request	to motivate	to recommend
to report findings	to respond	to praise
to inform	to propose	to announce

Very few memos are only informational. Usually, you want to get the reader to act, or at least to agree with you. If you find yourself answering "to inform" repeatedly, take a second look. Have you analyzed your purpose carefully enough? Have you stated it as precisely as possible?

AUDIENCE

In analyzing your audience, you may consider questions such as:

- Is my audience likely to be receptive, indifferent, or resistant?
- If there are several readers, will their reactions differ?
- How technical can I be?
- Will my audience recognize acronyms?
- Should I "soft-pedal" the request, or should I be assertive?

BOTTOM LINE

What is the one idea you want the reader to remember? The sooner you can boil your message down to one or two sentences, the easier it will be to write. If you are having trouble doing this, continue with the process, then return to this question after Step 2.

The bottom line is often more subtle than you would expect. For example, when you are announcing a meeting, the bottom line is probably not "I'm holding a meeting." It's more likely to be "this meeting is vital and I need you there!" Don't always go with your first idea. Careful analysis will pay off.

STRATEGY

Make sure you are correct in the timing of your communication. Should you send it today? In a week? Also ask yourself if you are the person who should be doing the writing. Could a phone call or other method of communicating be better? What about a meeting, a telegram, or even a cassette tape?

We often see managers writing much too late to solve problems. Be sure you haven't lost your opportunity to deal with the situation. Writing after the fact wastes your time and the readers' time, and lowers your credibility.

When you determine your strategy, you may decide to build in some accountability, such as:

Please return this form by 3:00 P.M., Wednesday, June 9.

Just keep in mind what results you want and make your requests as clear as possible. Of course, your timing is essential. For example, you might be defeating your

FOCUS SHEET

1. **Purpose**
   - Why am I writing this? *To report on search for plant relocation site in the state.*
   - What do I want the reader to do? *To approve expanding the search and consider re-locating out-of-state.*

2. **Audience**
   - Who is/are my reader(s)? *Vice president for facilities and operations, chief executive officer; possibly the board of directors.*
   - What is the reader's role? *They all control high level decisions and have a say in the budget.*
   - What does the reader know about the subject? *The vice president is knowledgeable; the CEO and board of directors — not much.*
   - How will the reader react? *They're all going to question the costs of out-of-state re-location & make me justify it to the last penny. The CEO & Board may be resistant because relocation may mean losing tax benefits.*
   - What is my reader's style? Should I adjust to it? *They're too busy to do this study themselves. They want all the information as concise as possible. I'd better keep this brief and fact-filled.*
   - How will the reader use this document? *They need evidence that we need to re-locate and that an out-of-state location, the costs, are justifiable.*
   - Whom should I include in this mailing? *Everyone on the relocation committee.*

3. **Bottom line**
   - If the reader were to forget everything else, what one key point do I want the reader to remember? *We need to begin exploring immediately the prospects of opening our next facility out-of-state. After seven weeks of interviews with state and local development officials, I believe we are one year from seriously being able to consider an expansion here. It would take us no more time to explore out-of-state options, so we have nothing to lose. I would be happy to undertake the out-of-state search.*

4. **Strategy**
   - Should *I* be writing this? At *this* time? *Yes.* Would a phone call or meeting be more effective? *No.*
   - Should I send this at all? Am I too late? *I don't see any risk in sending it. We are stuck in our expansion plans and whether my idea is pursued or not, it shows a creative approach.*
   - Is someone else communicating this same information? Should I check with that person? *No, this is my responsibility. But I will ask Sam in Finance if he received the tax information I sent for.*
   - Should I include deadlines? Actions requested? *Probably. I'll have a better idea of the timing after I speak with Sam tomorrow.*
   - Is my method of transmission the best? Should I be using the traditional mail? *I'll hand deliver this by next Monday.*

purpose if you submit a controversial proposal an hour before your boss leaves for a vacation. Or you could be helping your cause if you present it shortly after the boss has received praise for his trend-setting management techniques.

Sample: A completed Focus Sheet

This is how one manager used the Focus Sheet to get started with a writing project.

Continuing the process

Now that you have a strong sense of your audience and purpose, you are ready to continue with Step 2, "Generate Ideas with a Start-up Strategy."

In the next chapter, you will find some strategies to help you pull your thoughts together, even when you're not quite sure what you want to say. Some of the ideas are new; others have helped writers for years. In all our writing workshops, at least one of these strategies has transformed a despairing writer into a born-again writer, undaunted by the next memo deadline.

Generate Ideas with a Start-up Strategy

Getting started is, for most of us, the hardest part of writing. But it need not be. The Better Communications Start-up Strategies help writers develop a more positive attitude toward the beginning phases of writing.

MANAGE YOUR WRITING TIME

Do you sometimes try to write a first draft before you've created a plan? The old "ready, fire, aim" approach? Habits like that are time-consuming. As you'll see, writing the first draft will be easier if you do Steps 1 through 5 first. Invest time in planning. It will make your actual writing and editing faster and easier. Engineers make sketches before they start drafting. Efficient business writers must plan the same way.

Generating ideas

First, you need to put all of your ideas down on paper where you can look at them. Those great ideas you have while taking a shower, when driving to work, or before falling asleep can be forgotten or discounted until written down. In fact, all the Start-up Strategies are aimed at making sure you store your ideas, not in your head, but on paper, where they belong.

In some situations, you are the expert. You know the problem you're facing; you know the possible solutions. The ideas are there; you just need to concentrate on their presentation. In other instances, you may have to do some research, speak with colleagues or consultants, analyze data, meet with clients, or understand user requirements.

Putting your ideas on paper, you can:
- see if your information is complete
- decide what to include and what to leave out
- organize an effective presentation

Match the strategy to the task

Different writing projects require different start-up techniques. For a short letter, you may need to jot down only a quick list. Longer documents will almost always require more extensive planning. Begin with a short letter or memo—and after you've mastered that, move on to more elaborate reports and proposals.

Remember: as difficult as it is for most people to conquer the blank page or screen, things flow a lot more smoothly if you use one of these Start-up Strategies:

Traditional Outline	Index Cards
Questioning	Movable Post-it Tape or Notes
Brainstorm Outline	Free Writing
Starting at the Computer	Dictating (as a Start-up Strategy)

THE TRADITIONAL OUTLINE
(For All Types of Writing)

Although many of our clients say that writing a Traditional Outline fills them with dread, we meet one or two in every workshop who say that this tried-and-true method works perfectly well for them. If you're one of the lucky ones who can easily envision a plan for your document, keep using the classic outline. You might also want to skip ahead to Step 3.

Using the Traditional Outline

On page 16 is a sample outline for a proposal to purchase a laser printer. In its simplest form, an outline is a list of ideas you want to include in your writing—arranged in a coherent order. If you can generate a "quick and dirty" list or outline, you don't need any other Start-up Strategies.

The seven other strategies offered here are in fact pre-outline techniques to bring you to the final outline stage. They are all designed to spark a group of ideas you can then put in the best order (see Step 4). Whether you wish to take these ideas one step further by copying them into traditional outline form is up to you. If you do so, remember to indicate in some way the difference between main ideas and sub-ideas.

Here are a few ways to do that:

A SAMPLE TRADITIONAL OUTLINE
TO PROPOSE PURCHASE OF A LASER PRINTER

    I. Overview

   II. Why do we need a laser printer?

  III. Benefits of the laser printer
- A. Saves time
  1. No need to wait for printer's deliveries
  2. Documents can be updated instantly
- B. Saves cost of typesetting
- C. Makes camera-ready copy
- D. More creative use of personnel

  IV. Experiences of other users
- A. Company X
- B. Company Y
- C. Company Z

   V. Potential vendors
- A. Ace
- B. Acme
- C. Apex

  VI. Costs
- A. Financing
- B. The equipment
- C. Installation
- D. Training of personnel

 VII. Implementation timetable
- A. Space allocation
- B. Installation schedule
- C. Training schedule (personnel)

VIII. Background
- A. Other investigations on this issue
- B. Current equipment on hand

  IX. Long-term plans
- A. Options to upgrade
- B. Potential applications

   X. Summary

(1) Use *A*'s and *B*'s contrasted with Roman and Arabic numerals—the traditional approach.

(2) Mark main ideas with a special sign, such as a circle (or bullet), a star, or an X. (• * X)

(3) Write main ideas in one color and less important ideas in a contrasting color. Use three colors if the list/outline is very complex.

QUESTIONING (For Memos and Letters)

With a completed Focus Sheet, you have a clearer picture of your readers, their needs and their expectations. Using that reader profile, you can engage your audience in an imaginary dialogue.

How does questioning work?

Questioning is very similar to role-playing, except that the writer plays both parts.
(1) List questions your readers will need answered about your topic. Include such issues as background, requirements, features, benefits, changes, costs, alternatives, and timing.
(2) Write answers under each of the questions. Respond to each one as completely as possible: you can cut and refine the information later.

If you can't answer all the questions, you may need more information before you can go further. Using the Questioning Strategy as a starter can spare you more research after you've begun to write, or the embarrassment of distributing an incomplete document.

For example, suppose you are drafting a memo announcing a new monthly department meeting. What are some of the questions your reader will ask?
- What will be on the agenda?
- How can I prepare for the meeting?
- Am I *required* to go?
- What if I can't make it?

Answer the questions you've generated and you're on your way.

THE BRAINSTORM OUTLINE (For Long Memos and Reports)

"How can I possibly keep track of all my ideas?"

The Brainstorm Outline allows you to pour out all your ideas without committing yourself in advance as to their relative importance or to the order in which you will ultimately present them. After you have mapped your ideas on the Brainstorm Outline, it is far easier to move on to a Traditional Outline, if you like. If you find yourself thinking, *I have so many ideas, I just don't know how to begin,* the Brainstorm Outline is for you.

What is a Brainstorm Outline?

A Brainstorm Outline is a nonlinear, pictorial way of getting your ideas and their relationship to each other on paper. The Brainstorm Outline goes beyond the traditional outline—it opens you up to a spontaneous way of thinking. It is especially helpful for writing problem-solving memos because it encourages free association and provides lots of space on the outline for squeezing in new ideas. With this strategy, all your ideas are displayed at once so you can easily see their relationship to each other. Similar thoughts are grouped together. After you have completed the outline, you can then decide which ideas are most important by numbering them in the order that you want to discuss them. If you like, you can copy them later into an easy-to-follow list or outline.

On page 19 is a sample Brainstorm Outline for a memo requesting the purchase of a faster laser printer.

How to plan a report or memo using a Brainstorm Outline

In the center of a large piece of plain white paper (minimum size: 8½″ × 11″), draw a circle big enough to contain six or seven words. In the circle, write the main goal of your memo or report. This will probably begin with a phrase such as:

to persuade	to analyze	to explain
to report findings	to request	

Now draw a line extending out like the spoke of a wheel in any direction from the circle. As close as possible to the line, jot down an important idea that you want to include in your writing. It doesn't matter whether this is the idea you want to mention first or last in the final draft. Group ideas about the same subject along the same spoke or one emerging from it. List all ideas as they occur to you, as quickly as you can. Try to keep the momentum going. The Brainstorm Outline will look like a wheel with many spokes.

Continue adding more spokes for different thoughts. As you write each idea, ask yourself whether it deserves a new spoke of its own or whether it should be an offshoot of an already existing spoke.

When all your thoughts are on the spokes, you can choose an order for presenting them in the actual memo. After studying Step 4 on sequence (page 43), number the spokes in the order that seems best. When a group of words seems to hang together as one section, you can circle that area and put a number within the circle. If the outline is quite complex, you may want to circle numbered areas in different-colored inks.

REMEMBER: (1) Put ideas that are related on the same spoke or close to it.

(2) Let the less important facts stem out of the more important ones.

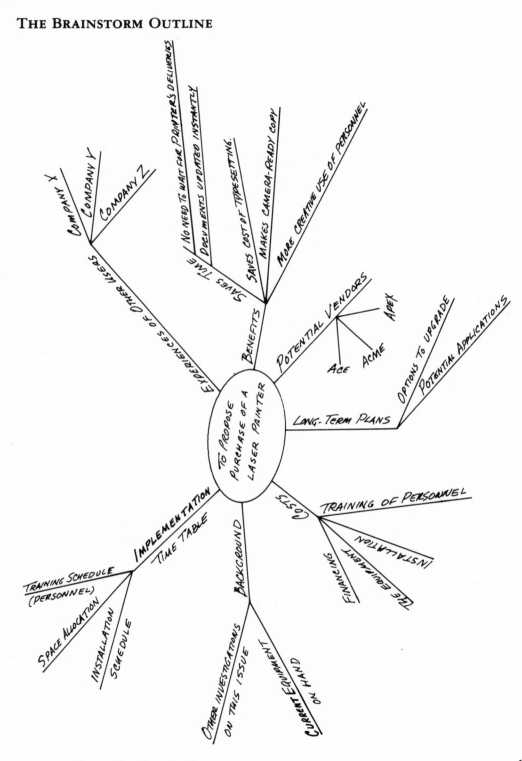

Page 23 shows how I sequenced my ideas on this Brainstorm Outline (though you may have chosen another, equally good solution).

ON YOUR OWN: Using the Brainstorm Outline below, plan a memo suggesting a change in one of your company procedures that you believe would improve your working atmosphere.

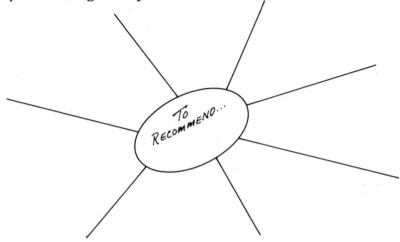

STARTING AT THE COMPUTER

Imagine what it would be like to see your ideas in front of you almost as soon as they occur to you. How would it feel to write as fast as your fingers can go? What if carriage returns and correction fluid were never again an issue? Or sharpened pencils? Or lined pads? Just have an idea, and there it is—before your eyes.

Before explaining more of our traditional manual techniques for getting started, let's look at using word-processing technology in the start-up stage. As you know if you're already using one, computers can help you both generate and manage the information you want to convey. Several tips follow for using your computer to get your ideas down quickly. After each tip, we list the manual versions of the technique, which are explained later in this section. So boot up and let's begin.

As always, start with your Focus Sheet

With your filled-out Focus Sheet before you, you've already begun. As we discussed in Step 1, the Focus Sheet contains profiles of your audience and purpose. These in turn have given you your strategy point—the point your document must make to achieve your purpose. Now it's time to generate some content that will support or develop that point or bottom line.

One size doesn't fit all

No single noncomputerized Start-up Strategy works for every writing project. For one thing, each project differs in familiarity and scope. You write some things routinely; others take some thinking about.

But your computer can help in all cases. Regardless of the situation, your computer can eliminate much of the time and drudgery associated with gathering and organizing information for any writing project. Whether you work a little at a time, jotting down ideas when they hit you, or write an entire document at one sitting, the computer will speed up the process.

Tip #1: For short or medium length documents, use Screen Outlining

Computers allow you to manipulate the sequence of information very easily. For this reason, the traditional outline on the screen is much less restrictive and far more practical than it was in Miss Groundgripper's eighth-grade English class.

A modern, computer adaptation of outlining is easy to master: Assemble in front of you the types of information this document demands. Then use either the Questioning technique described on page 17 or the Brainstorm Outline, also explained on page 17.

QUESTIONING Using the Questioning technique, type the questions you formulate into your computer. Then answer each question to create a rough predraft.

THE BRAINSTORM OUTLINE This is a planning strategy you can work on anywhere, using even the back of an envelope or napkin. Before you sit down at your computer, try a Brainstorm Outline for your project. Then put the outline in front of you when you use your favorite word-processing program. Transfer the information from your Brainstorm Outline to the screen in Traditional Outline form or randomly, whichever seems easier. Use your word processor's insertion capability to fill in details, ideas, data, steps, and events, under your screen-outline topics.

Warning! Do not worry at this point about the sequence of either your topics or your details. The objective here is just to get a "brain-dump" of ideas out on the screen.

Tip #2: When organizing lots of information, use Data Files

Take advantage of your computer's storage capacity to cope with more complicated projects. Instead of keeping all of your information in one file, open a new file for each section and either brainstorm or enter your details. Save each file on the same disk for easier retrieving and merging later. Also, assign similar names for each file that will be part of the same document, so that the index of your disk can group them for you. Then, either print a draft of each file or use merging techniques to decide how it all fits together.

If you do a lot of complex documents, consider purchasing integrated programs which allow easy transfer of information between their three components: database, word processing, and spreadsheet functions.

Tip #3: When you have several ongoing projects, use Clipboard Files

Some computer systems have clipboard files, or note pads. Use these for temporary storage of brief ideas that may not pertain to the disk you're using. Then "file" them later when you're working with the right disk.

Tip #4: Use automatic outliners

In Step 3, we cover automatic outliners as a way to organize information. They are also excellent devices for beginning any writing task.

Tip #5: A cure for writer's block: "Free Screening"

By simply turning down the light on your screen, you can turn off your internal critic when you input. As you stare at the darkened screen, use the Free-Writing Start-up Strategy to free you from worrying about grammar, spelling, punctuation, word choice, or sequence until it's time.

After you have drained your brain, turn up the light and see the results. Even if some of it doesn't make sense, you'll still have plenty of usable ideas.

ON YOUR OWN: Try writing a memo using one or more of the approaches we've described. Use a topic related to your job, or tackle this one: "If I could redesign any office system, I'd suggest . . ."

You don't own a laptop computer yet? Don't despair!

When you're away from your machine, you can switch back and forth between the computer and the manual techniques suggested in this chapter.

INDEX CARDS (For Long Reports)

Didn't you groan when you saw the teacher's pet smugly snap a rubber band around his term-paper index cards—at the same time you secretly wished you had followed his example?

If you don't have a word processor, index cards are the best Start-up Strategy for documents that require extensive research. Avoid a huge, unmanageable pileup of ideas and facts with this time-tested strategy. You can accumulate a large amount of material before deciding on a structure for presenting your message. You can shuffle the order of your ideas, discard irrelevant ones, and add afterthoughts without wasting valuable time and energy rewriting. Later you will arrange your information into a framework that will form the skeleton of your report. Right now you need only concern yourself with gathering the "bones" that will compose it.

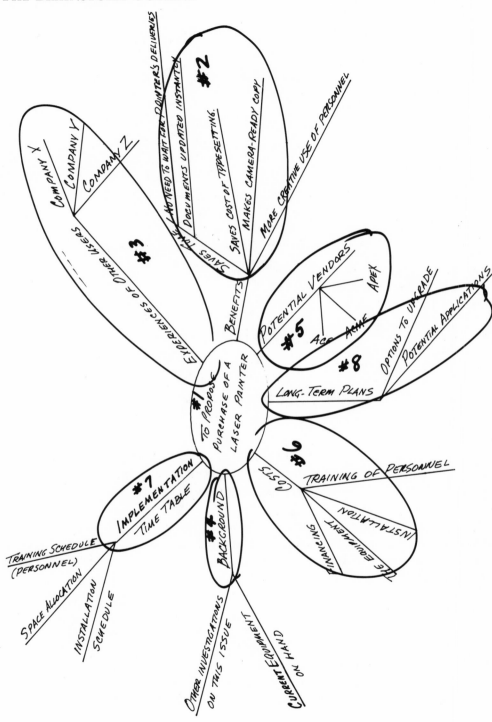

How to do it

STEP 1: Take all notes on cards, including free-written ideas and insights. (See discussion of free writing on page 25.) If you can express your idea in one sentence, don't feel you should add more information to the card. By limiting yourself to one idea per card, it will be easier to put the cards into the desired order later without rewriting. For lists of facts or statistics that take up more than one card, create your own system to key sections that belong together. A large color-coded dot in the upper right-hand corner works well.

STEP 2: Spread the cards out on your desk. Read through them and sort into piles according to similar topics. When you've finished, top off each pile with a "header card," so that you know the general contents of the piles by quickly glancing at the header. Put a rubber band around each pile.

STEP 3: Referring to your header cards, choose your Method of Development (see Step 4) and arrange your banded piles accordingly.

STEP 4: Look back through each pile to be sure you like the order of ideas contained under each header card.

You've quickly created a skeleton that will support the body of your project. By using this time-saving method for getting started, you can afford to spend more time working on paragraphs.

MOVABLE POST-IT TAPE OR NOTES (For Long Memos & Reports)

Post-it tape (manufactured by 3M) is a product all writers should consider for developing an outline. Packaged like a roll of cellophane tape, it is available at most stationery stores. You can write or type directly on the tape; you can also peel it up and move it around many times.

Write each idea for your outline on a separate piece of tape. You can then rearrange the strips as often as necessary—no need to rewrite, no messy crossing out, no confusing arrows, no tiny scribbles in the margins. If you prefer, you can also use the popular larger version: 3M's Post-it Note Pads, which are small pads of self-adhering paper. For people without a computer, this method works like a manual word processor.

How to plan a memo with the tape or notes

STEP 1: Cover a piece of paper with notes or strips of tape four to five inches long. Use each strip as you would an index card—to write notes, phrases and ideas that you want to include in your memo. Fill as many strips as you need to cover all your main points. Don't hesitate to put down any idea—no matter how unimportant. You can always weed it out later.

STEP 2: When you've finished note making, experiment with different Methods of Development by changing the order of the strips (see Step 4). Rearrange the strips until the most appropriate sequence emerges. Explore all possibilities.

STEP 3: As with index cards, you may want to color-code strips of tape for easy grouping. Related ideas should have the same colored dot or stripe on the left-hand edge of the strip. Offset subordinate ideas by indenting the strips of tape on the paper to make them resemble a traditional outline.

When you get to your first draft, write one paragraph for each idea-bearing strip. Some executives I've worked with are so enthusiastic about the tape that they use it for all note-taking occasions. By doing this faithfully, they always have instant outlines, ready to expand into full reports.

How to use movable tape or notes for editing

This versatile tape can also be helpful when it's time to edit your memo or report. Use the tape to insert additional ideas or to make changes in the original ones. If you want to make a minor change, place the tape in the margin. For a more substantial change, simply cover the section with the tape and start over again.

You also can use the tape to make editorial comments to others. If you don't want to mark directly on the original copy of someone else's report, place the tape in the margin and write on it. Your comments will be received as a useful aside that can be easily removed. Furthermore, if you yourself decide against a correction or comment, you can toss away the tape—not your report.

⤮ ON YOUR OWN: Using movable tape, write a memo dealing with this situation:

You recently interviewed a candidate for a job opening in your department. Write a memo evaluating the candidate's strengths and weaknesses. Do you recommend that the candidate be hired?

FREE WRITING (For All Types of Documents)

When to use it

From time to time, you may feel too blocked to make a plan or list of any kind. Perhaps you're so intimidated by what others will think of your writing that you get stuck. If this happens, try a special technique called Free Writing that is used by many professional writers to limber up.

How to do it

Free Writing is thinking on paper—putting down everything that comes to mind. As in free associating, the goal is to write down any and all ideas, whether or not they are related to your topic. Try not to stop—don't answer the phone, don't stop for a cup of tea, just keep writing—even if you find yourself swearing on paper or writing about things that are off the topic.

Don't worry about punctuation or word choice. Most of us have an "internal critic" who wants us to struggle with grammar and work at fine-tuning our sentences as we write them. Don't let that inner voice slow you down. Editing or censoring yourself at this stage would disrupt the flow of ideas. If you can't immediately find the word you need, leave a blank and go on. Forget about complete sentences for now; use fragments, phrases, whatever emerges. Just keep producing words.

How Free Writing helps

Letting your thoughts range widely on any issues that come to mind—even personal ones—opens the channels for what you are really trying to say. This process helps you transfer vague ideas circulating in your mind onto paper before they slip away. Once they are in black and white for you to read, others will soon follow.

Free Writing helps you get rid of distracting thoughts that may be interfering with the serious writing you are trying to produce. When your mind keeps returning to last night's yoga class or the fifty dollars Cousin Nelson owes you, it's better to let all those distractions spill onto the paper, too. Soon the bothersome thoughts will be released and your mind will feel clearer, ready for other tasks. If you remember an errand you must do later, such as picking up a loaf of bread on the way home, jot it down on a separate list. This, too, will liberate your mind.

Free Writing is, in a way, like meditating. It removes the pressure to create a perfect product: anything you write down is acceptable. The mere act of writing in a nonstop, unfettered way will give you the confidence that more and more thoughts will emerge. Suddenly, you have developed a rhythm. The pen is moving as if propelled across the page. This rhythm will stay with you—it gets you rolling the way warm-up exercises help you to jog or dance better.

Your plan seems to write itself

Free Writing almost effortlessly generates tangible material for you to work with. After allowing all your relevant and irrelevant thoughts to emerge quickly, you will find a good number of salvageable ideas among them. Take a red pen and circle passages or sentences that represent a useful idea. You may be grateful and surprised to see that three pages of Free Writing have yielded enough information to create the framework for your outline.

Ideas emerging from Free-Writing exercises can be transferred to other Start-up Strategies for further planning. Put words or phrases on a Brainstorm Outline, movable tape, index cards, or a Traditional Outline.

The outpouring below, from a confused and harried Hope Slater, helped her to pull her thoughts together and find a place to start. Looking back at her scribbling, Hope found some useful ideas in it. She circled every word or phrase that seemed salvageable and tried to group similar ideas by numbering them (page 34).

Hope used the Free-Writing exercise two more times, by which point she had generated enough ideas to make a good list of topics for her report. She also used the technique to develop some in-depth initial thinking on several of the ideas that emerged in her first Free-Writing effort. In the end, she had created a clear outline, ready to develop into a first draft.

ON YOUR OWN: Fill this sheet or the next with your thoughts on a work-related topic or with our suggested topic below. If you work on a PC or terminal, refer to "Starting at the Computer" in this section for suggestions on Free Screening. Give yourself ten minutes.

Suggested topic:

"If I could redesign my job in any way . . ." Write as quickly as you can, without concern for sentence structure or organization. Keep writing without stopping until your time is up.

HOPE'S FREE-WRITING WARM-UP

I can't believe it. Here I am chained again to my desk with this stupid report to write and my boss breathing down my neck to finish it. Why me? I'd much rather be at the sales conference shaking hands and hearing that keynote speaker—what was his name?—who's done so much research on building robots—the wave of the future—I can't wait to have my *own.*

Anyway . . . I'm getting warmed up here . . . maybe writing isn't so bad . . . using these dots between my words helps . . . I don't even have to think about punctuation . . . Anyway what's my topic? Oh yes . . . an analysis of text processing usage by different departments to see 1) if it's being used fairly, 2) to try to figure out if any one department is hogging it all, 3) to see if we may need to enhance the system soon because our needs seem to be growing so quickly, 4) is this really true or are people just squawking because they want instant access and service? Hmm that's a tall order. Where shall I start? Also, what about coming up with a fair amount of time that users should expect to wait for their processing? How to determine this?? Well I guess I could include the interviews I've collected from everyone plus the statistics on machine usage that Jamie gathered. What else? Maybe do my own survey of projected needs? I should be sure to ask about 1) projected staff increases, 2) new projects anticipated, 3) staff turnover requiring reorientation toward equipment and usage procedures. Oh it's so hard to concentrate on this. I wonder if it's raining out. Did I take that steak out of the freezer for tonight?—oooh I'd better call Betty and see. But no, I must not allow distractions. I promised myself I'd keep writing for twenty minutes no matter what happened. Let's see what else can I put into my report?

DICTATING AS A START-UP STRATEGY

Dictating is a form of Free Writing. Instead of writing down whatever comes to mind, you *say* whatever comes to mind. Free Writing lets you "see what you think," and dictating lets you "hear what you think." It gets the ideas onto the air-waves, and gives you a chance to sort through your random, unorganized thoughts.

Just speak-write into the microphone

Turn on the "record" button and say what's on your mind. Whether your thoughts are on-topic or off-topic, this Start-up Strategy will be useful. Remember, the point is to get warmed up. Don't censor your ideas, and don't stop talking. You'll be surprised to find how many half-formulated yet valuable ideas lurk in the corners of your brain. Time yourself, and see how much you can say in five uninterrupted minutes.

To type or not to type

Dictating alone, without preparing a transcript from the tape, may be helpful enough that you can move immediately to another Start-up Strategy and write down some of the ideas you've uncovered.

But you'll probably want to look at a typed version and use that as a starting point. Have your typist triple-space the text, so you have plenty of room to add notes. Some people even cut and paste sections to reorganize ideas just as if they were using 3 × 5 cards. Find what works for you.

WRITER'S BLOCK

The Blank Page (or Screen) Syndrome

The chart that follows summarizes the Start-up Strategies we've covered and also gives suggestions for matching each strategy to your particular "Blank Page Syndrome." Check the list of "symptoms" to find which apply to you, then try the "remedy." Also feel free to use the strategy that appeals to you most. Match your strategy to your personality.

What to do when you're so blocked you're desperate

The Beatles had the right idea when they sang, "I get by with a little help from my friends." When all else fails, find someone with a bit of extra time who is willing to help you. Explain that you're struggling with writer's block and that talking over your writing project would help you tremendously.

Using your Focus Sheet as a guide, take notes or, with permission, tape-record the conversation. Mention every possible idea you're thinking of including. Ask the person to listen carefully and to question you when something needs clarification.

THE BLANK PAGE OR SCREEN SYNDROME
or Choosing the Right Start-up Strategy

SYMPTOM	REMEDY
• You just don't know where to start.	Use the *Questioning Strategy.* Ask yourself the questions your readers will ask.
	OR
	Use *Free Writing.* Just start writing and don't stop until all your ideas are on paper. Let yourself free-associate. Edit later.
• You need to organize and convey a large amount of information and overlook nothing.	Use the *Brainstorm Outline* format. Then number areas in logical order to create your particular outline.
	OR
	Use *index cards* or *movable tape* or notes. List ideas, then organize.
• You are taking notes in the field, interviewing many people. You are covering many subjects.	Organize with *movable tape.* Put all of your notes on tape, then arrange them in order to create an outline.
• You're agonizing over your first draft, trying to make it perfect.	Use the *Free Writing* approach.
• You know exactly what you want to say and have a clear plan in mind.	Use the *Traditional Outline.*

Later, play back the tape. You can enter the information directly into your word processor or take notes—on movable notes or tape for short material, 3 × 5 cards for a long report. Add other information that has occurred to you in the meantime.

A different approach to beating writer's block

(1) Change environment—find a quiet place with no distractions.
(2) Ask a coworker to take a look at your work. Outside suggestions help.
(3) Make a checklist of tasks that you still must complete. Check them off so you can *see* your progress.
(4) Skip to another section that you know you can write.
(5) Take a break. Leave it for a while. Get up and stretch. Walk around. Jog. Dance. Get distance. Come back to the job refreshed, with a positive attitude.

STEP THREE
Group Information Under Headlines

You've generated good information in Step 2. Now it's time to group related ideas into categories. Once you've done that, you will be ready to sequence the information (Step 4) and to write your first draft (Step 5).

GROUP IDEAS BY CATEGORY

What is a category? Think of a refrigerator. Each section is for a different category of food: cheese goes in the dairy bin, and lettuce goes in the vegetable bin. What would happen if you looked in the fruit bin and found the ice cream? You'd find a disaster. Whoever unpacked the groceries didn't put things in the right categories. It's your job to organize the information in your intended document so that the reader won't find Background Information—like melting ice cream—in the Recommendations section.

Creating categories: what are your choices?

Once you start thinking about grouping information, you'll notice that there are countless possibilities. However, the same general categories for organizing information prove to be useful again and again, no matter what type of company we visit. Information seems to fall into predictable categories that we call *generic* categories. Here are a few samples:

Statement of purpose   Request for action
Proposal   Rationale for action
Announcement of a change   Background information

Directions, Instructions	Observations
Explanation of a process or procedure	Scope of investigation
Results of a study	Analysis of findings
Explanation of cause	Evaluation
Expression of thanks	Implementation plan
Conclusions	Recommendations
Description of a situation	Considerations
Sequence of events	Introduction of a new idea

© 1983 Deborah Dumaine

Sample generic categories for documents

The lists on pages 32–33 will help you identify the generic categories commonly used for business documents and may serve as a jumping-off point for your own projects. The lists are not a substitute for your own serious analysis of the information you want to convey. Use them instead as models of effective organization.

HOW TO GROUP IDEAS FROM YOUR START-UP STRATEGY

If you used a *Traditional Outline* in Step 2, you'll have a head start on Step 3. Your ideas are already grouped together. At most, you'll probably find yourself adding subcategories under the Roman numerals or letters.

If you used *index cards* or movable tape or Post-it Notes sort your ideas into piles or groups of similar or closely related ideas. Perhaps several of your ideas relate to "reasons for a takeover now." Group all of them together. Other ideas may be part of the implementation plan; group them in a separate place.

For each pile or group, think of a one- to four-word "bin"—a category like the ones suggested earlier that will "hold" your ideas. Write that category on a tape strip or index card and attach it at the top of your list of movable-tape strips or to the top of your group of index cards.

If you chose the *Brainstorm Outline* as your Start-up Strategy, you did much of your clustering as you brainstormed. The "branches" of your outline are your main categories, while the "twigs" are the subcategories. As explained in Step 2, look for big-picture categories and draw circles around your major segments. If you need to include more than one branch in your circle, that's fine. See page 23 for a Brainstorm Outline with categories circled.

If you used *Free Writing* to start, you can organize your ideas as we have done in Hope's writing that follows:

Typical Categories for Common Memos & Reports

Meeting Announcement
1. Time and place of meeting
2. Agenda: a list of topics
3. Speakers
4. Background
   • events leading to calling of meeting
   • what you hope to accomplish
5. Information to consider
6. How to prepare for the meeting
7. Contact/person in charge

Decision-Needed Memo
1. Overview
2. Issue under consideration
3. Recommended action
   • who is involved in the "action"
   • schedule of steps to be taken
   • pros and cons
   • subsequent meetings
4. Background
   • why it became an issue
5. Other decisions/options
   • pros & cons for each
6. Results of study
7. Summary

Status Report
1. Executive summary
2. Project description
3. Current status: progress to date
4. Successful aspects
5. Problems encountered
6. Planned solutions
   • further information needed
   • opinion needed
   • decision needed
   • request for confirmation of plan
7. Other projects completed
   • summary of each
8. Other projects still in progress
   • background
   • status
   • forecast of
     (a) time schedule
     (b) changes
     (c) cost
9. Summary

Performance Analysis
1. Overview (of results)
2. Process or task analyzed
3. Problems detected
   • description of problems
   • possible causes of problems
4. Suggested solutions
   • people involved
   • cost (if any) involved
   • time involved
5. Comparison with previous model
   • similarities
   • differences
6. Dates for changes to be made
7. Date of next evaluation
8. Summary

Six Steps to Reader-Centered Writing

SOLVING A PROBLEM
1. Problem description
2. Recommended solution
3. Recommendation justified
4. Background
   • symptoms
   • causes

5. Alternative solutions
   • pros & cons
6. Implementation plan
7. Summary
   • problem restated
   • action requested (restated)

REQUEST TO PURCHASE
1. Overview
2. Recommendation (state what you want)
   • predicted productivity improvements
   • economic advantages
3. Analysis of items in question
   • cost justification
   • depreciation
   • brand selection

4. Implementation considerations
   • timetable
   • plan
5. Staffing requirements
6. Background
7. Summary

REQUEST FOR PROPOSAL
1. Overview
2. Service/item required
3. Background
   • relevant information
4. Possible problems

5. Budget considerations
6. Outline of response needed
7. Deadline for submission
8. Contact person
9. Summary

PROPOSAL
1. Abstract
2. The proposal stated
3. Supporting reasons
4. Plan
   • scope
   • schedule
   • budget
   • implementation

5. Points to investigate further
   • other people involved
   • time factors
6. Conclusions
   • restate recommendation/proposal
7. Summary

Group Information Under Headlines

1. Subdivide your writing into categories by circling ideas you want to use. Discard the rest.
2. Use colored circles to group closely related ideas.
3. Make a list of the categories on a separate piece of paper.
4. Pinpoint a word or phrase that categorizes each group. For example, is it a summary? A list of benefits? Write that word or phrase at the top of the appropriate group.

Hope's Free-Writing Warm-Up, with Ideas Circled

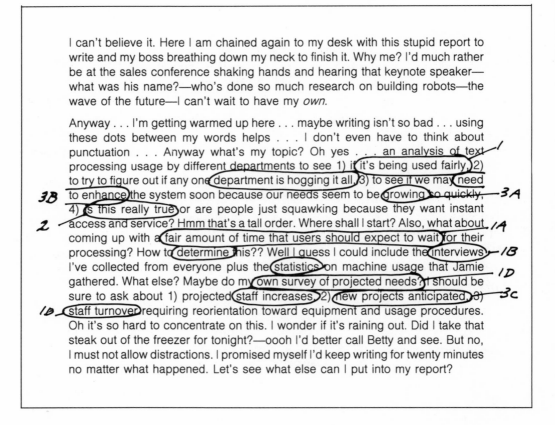

I can't believe it. Here I am chained again to my desk with this stupid report to write and my boss breathing down my neck to finish it. Why me? I'd much rather be at the sales conference shaking hands and hearing that keynote speaker— what was his name?—who's done so much research on building robots—the wave of the future—I can't wait to have my *own.*

Anyway . . . I'm getting warmed up here . . . maybe writing isn't so bad . . . using these dots between my words helps . . . I don't even have to think about punctuation . . . Anyway what's my topic? Oh yes . . . an analysis of text processing usage by different departments to see 1) if it's being used fairly, 2) to try to figure out if any one department is hogging it all, 3) to see if we may need to enhance the system soon because our needs seem to be growing so quickly, 4) is this really true or are people just squawking because they want instant access and service? Hmm that's a tall order. Where shall I start? Also, what about coming up with a fair amount of time that users should expect to wait for their processing? How to determine this?? Well I guess I could include the interviews I've collected from everyone plus the statistics on machine usage that Jamie gathered. What else? Maybe do my own survey of projected needs? I should be sure to ask about 1) projected staff increases, 2) new projects anticipated, 3) staff turnover requiring reorientation toward equipment and usage procedures. Oh it's so hard to concentrate on this. I wonder if it's raining out. Did I take that steak out of the freezer for tonight?—oooh I'd better call Betty and see. But no, I must not allow distractions. I promised myself I'd keep writing for twenty minutes no matter what happened. Let's see what else can I put into my report?

CREATE CATEGORIES WITH YOUR WORD PROCESSOR

One major benefit of having a word processor is the option of moving information around at the touch of a key. When you're creating categories, it's great to be able to delete a section and move it closer to related information. Grouping similar ideas is a breeze with this machine.

If you have inputted your first two steps' worth of information, you're ready to start clustering related ideas. Those who write long reports often keep all of their research in the computer. Using the "search" button, they can easily add new material to the section where it best fits.

Automatic outliners

If your word-processing package includes an outliner or if you have access to a separate outliner program, you're in luck. These wonderful programs allow you to view your document's outline in several valuable ways. For example, you can ask the outliner to display only the lines with Roman numerals or only the lines with capital letters. (See page 16 for an example of an outline.) If you decide to restructure your outline, the software will automatically renumber or re-alphabetize the entire list.

As you add to your document, the outline topics then become your headlines. When the document is quite long, you'll especially appreciate the outliner's ability to extract the outline instantly from the document so that you can examine its logic and structure. The longer the documents you write, the more you'll love outliners. No matter which Start-up Strategy you use, you'll end up with a list of categories. This is in fact a rough outline, ready to be fleshed out and put into sequence.

USE HEADLINES: GO PUBLIC WITH YOUR CATEGORIES

By clustering and organizing your ideas, you've built a framework for your document just as if you were building the frame of a house. The next task is to use that framework or outline to help your readers. Rather than making them guess whether they are reading the Background or the Problem Statement, share your outline. Translate your generic categories into specific headlines designed to guide your readers through your document.

First, what is a headline?

The five words you just read are a headline. They illustrate the content of the paragraph that follows by converting general categories to more specific and informative words. The primary difference between categories and headlines is that headlines are used as a device in a written document, and they are often more specific. "Background" as a headline wouldn't be as helpful as "We've never had a policy on early retirement."

While categories tend to be universal, it would be boring if all documents repeated the same headlines you see on pages 32 and 33. It's much more helpful to readers if we replace generic labels with catchy and specific titles that accurately reflect the content of the paragraph.

Headlines meet the same need that computers were invented to meet: the need to organize large amounts of information meaningfully. Computers use labels and categories to help the user key into the data they offer. Because all categories are carefully labeled and stored, one can call up information for review at a moment's notice. Headlines serve the same function—they allow the reader easy access to the information in a report or memo. Out of sheer necessity, headlining is rapidly becoming the writing approach for this decade.

Are they necessary for every report and memo?

Most emphatically, yes. Today's readers are too busy and distracted to read every word carefully. Headlines show readers what is important to them. They are the natural solution to the overwhelming amount of information that crosses our desks daily—what Alvin Toffler called "information overload."

See for yourself how headlines help

Two memos follow this paragraph. Don't read them; just glance at them. Which do you like better?

DATE: June 23, 1999
TO: All editorial and production unit chiefs
FROM: Ed Dittor, Managing Editor, *The Daily Muse*
RE: Meeting to discuss installing VX-40 video display equipment

The Zap Video Company has made an intriguing presentation to the publisher that we update the newsroom with the latest video display equipment. The publisher had asked me to discuss the proposal with other top staff for their opinions.

There will be a meeting in my office on June 30, 1999, at 10:00 A.M. If you cannot attend, let me know within two days whom you will be sending in your place.

Zap feels that we will be able to buck the trend of declining revenue if we convert to its VX-40 video display system. They say that our productivity will increase dramatically, our paper will run with fewer typographical mistakes, and that it's a proven morale booster for writers, editors, and the production staff.

Zap is aware of our weak financial situation. They, on the other hand, are in a good cash position at the moment and are willing to offer us excellent financing terms if we can quickly decide to go with their system. The company has given us two months to act.

There are several advantages in converting to the VX-40. To start with, writers will be able to get their copy out more quickly, once they become familiar with the system. Copy editors will also be able to do their job faster from the cleanly displayed version of stories that they will see. Edited stories can be sent to the production room instantly by pushing a button, thus reducing the time writers and editors will spend going up and down the stairs to the production room.

Gradually, we will be able to put our library on the system and code stories by writer, headline, first paragraph, or whole story. This is likely to mean that our writers will get more research done with much greater speed. (For description of other advantages, see the enclosed Zap Video promotional material.)

We do expect some problems, however, in converting to the VX-40. There will be significant union opposition to conversion. There's no other way to look at it: this means a loss of jobs, especially on the production side. Another factor we must also consider is financing. We will run up added costs in other areas; for example, new work desks must be purchased, and the whole building will have to be rewired. I need to know your thoughts on this proposal before the meeting. Every operation will be in for a serious interruption while people are training in the use of the new equipment.

DATE: June 23, 1999
TO: All editorial and production unit chiefs
FROM: Ed Dittor, Managing Editor, *The Daily Muse*
RE: Meeting to discuss installing VX-40 video display equipment

Purpose of meeting

The Zap Video Company has made an intriguing presentation to the publisher that we update the newsroom with the latest video display equipment. The publisher has asked me to discuss the proposal with other top staff for their opinions.

Meeting information

Where: My office
When: June 30, 1999, 4:00 P.M.

Actions requested

1. If you cannot attend, let me know by June 25th whom you will be sending in your place.

2. Please submit in writing any thoughts you have about Zap's proposal. I'd like to hear from you by June 25th at 5:00 P.M.

Zap Video's view of the benefits

Zap feels that we will be able to buck the trend of declining revenue if we convert to its VX-40 video display system. They say that productivity will increase dramatically and that morale will improve among editorial and production staff.

Importance of a quick decision

Zap is aware of our weak financial situation. They, on the other hand, are in a good cash position at the moment. They are willing to offer us excellent financial terms if we act within two months.

Advantages of converting to the VX-40 system

- Writers will get their copy out more quickly once they become familiar with the system.
- Copy editors will work faster from text cleanly displayed on the screen.
- Writers and editors won't waste time hand carrying copy to the production room since edited stories are instantly transmitted.
- Writers will spend their research time more efficiently because our library will be on the system. Stories can be coded by writer, headline, first paragraph, or whole story.
- The paper will run with fewer typographical errors.

See the enclosed Zap promotional material for a description of other advantages.

Disadvantages of converting to video

- We can expect the union to oppose conversion because it will mean a loss of jobs.
- Conversion is expensive. We must purchase new work desks and rewire the entire building.
- Every operation will be interrupted while people are learning the new equipment.

Which did you prefer?

You probably chose the second memo. Headlines, white space, and bullets create a dramatic visual impact. (I'll explain more about this in Step 6.) Equally important, however, is that *content* has more impact when you use headlines.

Headlines help the reader get the message

Headlines make ideas leap off the page. Notice how the headlines in this book speed up your reading. Thanks to headlines, readers who are in a hurry can skim through a memo or report and zero in on the section that interests them. Although you may have toiled over every sentence, your readers may not want to read everything you've written.

Headlines make information easier to find

Readers are generally looking for something specific. It is your job to help them find it. Headlines make it easier for your readers to find the section that applies to them or to relocate on second reading a section they found particularly important.

Think how grateful you would be to find in the files a well-headlined report on a subject you're researching. You could sift through it instantly to find the helpful ideas. Readers appreciate it when the information they are looking for is easy to find, just as if they were reading the morning paper. Can you imagine a newspaper written without headlines?

What about headlines on letters?

Headlines are becoming more popular in letter writing, but you will have to decide whether they are appropriate for your specific purpose and audience. Introducing memo-like headlines may violate the personal quality of some letters. However, headlines add clarity and directness to business letters.

Readers prefer headlined letters

Have you ever heard anyone complain about a well-designed document? We never have; we only hear about the ones that are badly designed. More and more of our clients agree that letters, like reports and memos, need attention to visual presentation. The headlined letter is a good example of an effective presentation:

October 20, 1996

Ms. Patty Partier
Orlando World Center
World Center Drive
Orlando, FL 32831

Re: Confirmation of 1998 reservations

Dear Patty:

Thanks for reminding us of our 1998 Orlando reservation. You are always so efficient and well organized; it's great to work with you. The information below will confirm our phone conversation.

Confirmation of show dates

Babbit & Babbit will hold part of our 1998 Introduction Show at the Orlando World Center from August 15 through September 5.

Action requested:

Please reserve our space on a 24-hour basis for these dates:

- both ballrooms—8/9 through 9/5
- other meeting rooms—8/12 through 9/5.

Next step: January site inspection

We will inspect hotel and convention center facilities in early January. Joe Smith and Diane Jones of our Training and Communications Department will call you soon to make an appointment. After we see the site, we will negotiate a contract with you.

Deadline for changes

Please call me by November 1st if you have any questions or would like to make any changes. Joe, Diane, and I are all looking forward to working with you to make this event another "smashing" success.

Thanks again, Patty, for your help.

Sincerely,

Walter Rosen

Should you write a letter or memo?

Sometimes you need both. If your letter starts expanding to a second page, it's usually a signal that you should write a short letter to cover personal messages only. Then attach a well-headlined memo for the business issues.

Use a subject line to begin memos, brief reports, and letters

A good "subject line" or "Re:" line answers the reader's first question: "What's this all about?" Later, it helps the reader recall the contents at a glance. Enormously useful to readers, subject lines can be used in letters just as they are in memos and reports. They are placed just beneath the address, before the salutation. Again, decide whether announcing your topic this way suits your audience and purpose.

Can I use my categories as headlines?

Yes. Sometimes the generic category is an excellent choice. If your "Re:" line already tells people the specific topic, "Background" may be all you need. For example, "Creating a personnel policy on early retirement" as a "Re:" line makes "Background" a perfectly informative headline later in the memo.

But don't use *only* generic categories. To set yours apart from the other documents in your reader's in-box, avoid using ho-hum standard stuff.

Combine the generic with the specific

To give as much information as you can in the headline, it can be useful to include both the generic category and a specific tidbit. Here are two examples:

Background: Union growth in the South
Proposal: We need to hire a new staff accountant

Step 6 offers more instruction on rewriting headlines for impact. For now, let's try an exercise to make sure you've got the basics.

Practice writing headlines

Directions: To test your skill in categorizing information, write an appropriate headline in each blank space in the memo on page 42.

Now compare your answers with the ones that follow. Don't worry if they are not exactly alike. If your headlines seem to match in meaning, you're on the right track.

Problem: Absenteeism increasing
Study recommended
Implications: Why is this important?
Specific complaints or Results of questionnaire or Action taken
Summary or Conclusion or How can we help?

DATE: July 10, 1999
TO: Vice President, Planning Division
FROM: Vice President, Human Resources
SUBJECT: Possible correlation between employee health and physical environment in the Jarvis Wing

A recent study of absenteeism revealed a 23% increase in midday illness and afternoon sick leave during the past ten months. The increase occurs exclusively in the four departments that moved ten months ago from the main building to the newly constructed Jarvis Wing.

The Personnel Division requests that the Planning Division undertake the immediate study of the Jarvis Wing. This situation is urgent. We suggest that the study include investigation of noise level, lighting level, light fixtures, and other outlets. The study should search for potentially toxic substances in or emissions from insulation, wall, floor and ceiling materials, and air circulation systems in the Jarvis Wing.

- This company is legally responsible for providing a safe work environment for its employees.
- The operation and productivity of this company depend on the efficient functioning of the departments located in the Jarvis Wing.
- Heads of the departments report decreases from levels of efficiency and accuracy prior to the move.

In response to the study of absenteeism, this department circulated a health questionnaire among employees in the four departments now located in the Jarvis Wing. The questionnaire revealed the following specific physical complaints:

- headache or migraine
- unusual eye fatigue
- general fatigue
- impaired ability to concentrate.

The complaints identified by the health questionnaire strongly suggest that something is wrong in the work environment and that further study of the problem is absolutely necessary. The Personnel Department is ready to help. My staff and I will be available to you as needed. Please let me know by this **Friday** what plans are in place to proceed with the study.

In conclusion

You've clustered your ideas into generic categories and assigned headlines to each category. Now let's move on to Step 4—how to sequence your sections for best result.

STEP FOUR
Sequence Your Ideas

One of the most challenging tasks of the writing process is sequencing: putting your ideas in the best order for impact. When you've chosen the appropriate method of development, your readers will be drawn to your ideas.

CHOOSE A METHOD OF DEVELOPMENT

All writers need to package their ideas logically. Step 3 covered the framework of the package. Step 4 covers the sequence of ideas within the package. Your Focus Sheet will help you choose a Method of Development (M.O.D.), which then determines the sequence of your paragraphs. Here are the most common Methods of Development:

1. Order of importance
   a. Most important to least important
   b. Least important to most important
2. Chronology
3. Process
4. Organization in space
5. Comparison/Contrast
6. Specific to General *or* General to Specific
7. Analysis

Some of these M.O.D.'s may overlap a bit, or you may find yourself using them in combination. This is perfectly acceptable.

Why is it essential to sequence your ideas strategically?

Clear writing is a sign of clear thinking. If you can put your thoughts together logically, your reader will more likely be convinced that you know what you're talking about. On the other hand, your mental disorganization will be quite obvious if it's splayed across a sheet of paper.

Now your hard work creating headlines pays off. If you hadn't categorized your ideas with headlines during Step 3, you would have difficulty sequencing them in Step 4. For example, how can you decide if Background goes toward the beginning or end of your report if you haven't defined that section by labeling it? This is why headlines are so helpful: they let you see your ideas for what they are.

How to choose a Method of Development

1. Review Steps 1 through 3. Remember when you pinpointed your "bottom line" on the Focus Sheet? From Step 1 on, you must keep in mind what you really want to accomplish. This is particularly vital in a memo about a controversial subject. Your key point could easily appear under any of the following headlines:

Conclusion	Action Requested
Recommendations	Next Steps
Deadline	Decision Needed

Look over the information you've accumulated on your Start-up Strategy (Step 2) and on your list of headlines.

2. Match your sequence to your audience's attitude. Ask yourself:

- Do I need to persuade my readers or do they already agree with my viewpoint?
- Which part of my message is most important? Least important?
- Do they need a neat summary, or is an in-depth analysis more appropriate?

In other words, choose a Method of Development according to the needs of your reader, your purpose for writing, the nature of your subject and your document, and the way your ideas naturally hang together.

M.O.D. #1: Order of Importance

A. Most important to least important

I begin with this method because it is the best organization for so many writing projects. You'll find it particularly useful in memos or reports that describe findings or offer important recommendations.

Below are segments that might appear in a typical two-page memo. They are arranged in order of importance, from most to least, using questions for headlines. The purpose of this memo is to persuade the reader (who is receptive to your suggestions) to adopt an ingenious new approach for improving efficiency in your department.

What are our current methods?	(description of situation)
How can we improve them?	(recommendation)
Why do we need this change?	(background/supporting data)
What are the benefits?	(convincers)
Can we implement the change?	(analysis)
What are the next steps?	(action items)

This sequence tells the reader a story—one with a beginning, a middle, and an end. With this logical presentation, the reader has not only a picture of the department's present status, but also a road map leading the department to greater efficiency.

Try this: What changes would make the following memo more persuasive?

DATE: May 25, 1999
TO: Joe Alton
FROM: Jean Dillon
RE: Budget Department

Since the budget and systems departments were split two months ago, systems personnel are no longer available to help out during peak times. In addition, the work load will be increasing. Corporate Headquarters has requested three new monthly reports in development, as well as new graphic exhibits.

Coverage must be maintained at all times because the budget department must supply information quickly and accurately to the Treasurer, general accounting, and other departments. Considering training classes, sick time, and vacations, this is virtually impossible with just two people in the department. Another accountant is needed in the budget department.

How did you do?

You're right if you put the last sentence in the memo first. In its current state, it's a mystery memo: the reader doesn't find the most important information until the end. On first reading, the memo seems like a history of the growth of personnel problems in the company.

What other changes did you make?

You probably added a headline for each paragraph; that would be a major improvement. Did you also use a more accurate subject line than "RE: Budget Department"? The introduction would have more impact if it said, "RE: The need to hire another accountant."

Remember: Whenever possible, put your most important information at the beginning of your writing, either in summary or in complete form.

> B.L.O.T. (Bottom Line On Top) has more impact than
> B.L.A.B. (Bottom Line At Bottom).

USEFUL FOR: Research reports, proposals, announcements, evaluations, status reports, procedural change notices, sales reports.

B. Least important to most important

Understanding your readers' attitudes is the key to successful writing. How will your readers react to your message? Sometimes your suggestion, request, or conclusion is just too controversial to use as an opener. Perhaps your memo proposes an unexpected solution to a problem, or a request for something already denied. Some readers can't handle a forthright, up-front request.

If you fear your readers will stop at the bad news, you will have to be more subtle by holding back your "bottom line" and laying the groundwork first. Perhaps you need "convincers" to lead the readers through your ideas until you bring them around to your point of view.

What if a manager named Rick had to introduce to his employees the upsetting idea of a time-card system? Look at his first attempt, the BEFORE memo that follows. Rick made two mistakes: (1) he arranged the information from most to least important from *his* viewpoint; (2) he emphasized *his* purpose and goal rather than his *readers'* concerns.

Next look at the AFTER memo. That one is arranged from least important to most important.

Which memo did you prefer?

Which would be most easily accepted? Which shows an understanding of people's psychological needs? In the second memo, the appealing and persuasive information is at the beginning, where it will be most effective. The second memo is clearly better.

Whether you present information from least to most important or most to least important can have major consequences. If a series of reasons will help the readers to understand your position, it is best to build from proof to proposition. You are leading your readers to your conclusion.

```
┌─────────────────────────────────────────────────────────────────────┐
│                                                                     │
│                            BEFORE                                   │
│                                                                     │
│   TO:      All manufacturing unit personnel                         │
│   FROM:    Rick Cotta                                               │
│   DATE:    April 21, 1999                                           │
│   RE:      Installation of time-card system                        │
│                                                                     │
│   Announcement                                                      │
│   As of May 1, 1999, Culture, Inc. will install a time-card system │
│   in the manufacturing unit. I am concerned that everyone is not    │
│   contributing an equal day's work for an equal day's pay. Most of  │
│   you are punctual and many put in more hours than we expect of     │
│   you. A few among you are not pulling your weight.                 │
│                                                                     │
│   New procedures                                                    │
│   Starting next month, all of you in the manufacturing unit will    │
│   record the actual number of hours you work each week on time      │
│   cards. The procedure is simple and takes less than thirty seconds │
│   each time you check in or out.                                    │
│                                                                     │
│   Why do we need more precise records?                              │
│   Management has two primary goals that cannot be met unless we     │
│   have better records of hours worked.                              │
│                                                                     │
│       1. We need to monitor productivity and efficiency accurately. │
│                                                                     │
│       2. We want to compensate people according to the number of    │
│          hours they work. (We recognize that some people work more  │
│          hours than expected, while others are paid the same for    │
│          coming in a little late and leaving a little early.)       │
│                                                                     │
│   Meeting planned                                                   │
│   I will announce a meeting soon so that we can discuss how the     │
│   time-card system will work and any concerns you may have.         │
│                                                                     │
│                                                                     │
└─────────────────────────────────────────────────────────────────────┘
```

Opinion-Reasons or Reasons-Opinion?

Whenever we consider the issue of most to least important, the question of how to present conclusions and evidence always arises. To present information persuasively, state your opinion or theory first, then prove it with supporting evidence. Your opinion will have more impact if the evidence that follows really upholds it.

To decide whether you should present opinion-reasons or reasons-opinion, consult your Focus Sheet. How did you answer the question, "How will the reader react?" Choose the appropriate presentation. Just be careful not to lose your proposition by burying it somewhere in the middle.

TO: All manufacturing unit personnel
FROM: Rick Cotta
DATE: April 21, 1999
RE: New personnel system

Changing needs

Over the years, Culture, Inc. has operated on a system of trust. We could easily see who was and who was not on the job. Now, because of our recent growth, it has become more difficult to keep track of employee hours.

Why do we need more precise records?

Management has two primary goals that cannot be met unless we have better records of hours worked.

1. We need to monitor productivity and efficiency accurately.
2. We want to compensate people according to the number of hours they work. Some people work longer hours than others. Paychecks should reflect that.

New tracking system starts next month

As of May 1, all of you in manufacturing will use a time card to record the number of hours you work each day. The procedure is simple, taking less than thirty seconds each time you check in or out.

Meeting planned

I will announce a meeting soon so that we can discuss how the time-card system will work and any concerns you may have.

A case history: What's the strategy here?

Should Mary Kennedy present her opinion first and reasons later, or vice versa? What does she really want to accomplish? Here's what happened:

For a long time, Mary and all the other top managers had felt that Rob Martinez deserved a promotion and a raise. His sales figures were the highest at Polytrix, and he had even started a sales training program to share his successful strategies.

Rob's friend Ed had recently hinted to Mary that Rob was feeling discontented at Polytrix, but no one believed he would actually leave. Then Mary found a copy of Rob's updated résumé in the copy machine and realized Ed knew more than he was telling. It was time to write a letter to the president to grant Rob the long-overdue promotion immediately.

In her memo, Mary chose to present her reasons first and her opinion last. Why? Because she knew that the president, who was on an austerity campaign, would not read beyond the words "salary increase." First, she had to alert him to Rob's possible resignation and remind him of his value to the company. Rob was too important an asset to lose.

In this way, Mary enticed the president into reading the entire contents of her startling memo. Had the economic state of the company been better and had the president been in a spending mood, Mary could have opened with her opinion and, with luck, secured Rob's promotion.

Summary: Test your sequencing ability

Try this brief review to be sure you're prepared to sequence your next document.

When my Audience is: *Put the Bottom Line:*

Receptive

                                               (where?)

Indifferent

                                               (where?)

Resistant

                                                 (where?)

Unknown

                                               (where?)

How did you do?

If your audience is receptive or unknown, put the bottom line on top. If your audience is indifferent, you have little to lose by stating your point first. If your audience is resistant, you then might want to pave the way tactfully to your point, but get there as soon as you can.

Workshop participants have told us that if they don't find the point immediately, they flip to the end anyway. So why hide your message?

Remember: Whenever possible, state your Bottom Line On Top, or as our trainers like to say, "B.L.O.T."

Audiences with mixed attitudes

If you have only one reader, it's fairly easy to determine the approach you should take. But what happens when you have two or more readers, and one of them loves your ideas, while the other reader is resistant? How do you then sequence your ideas?

If both readers have an equal role in the decision-making process, you will have to treat your audience as hostile and present your ideas accordingly. If, however, they are *not* both equally involved in the decision-making process, write for the decision makers, not the troublemakers.

Consider the end user

How is your document going to be used? Is the reader going to take action, or is she going to pass the memo along to someone who may then give it to someone else? If this is the case, be sure you address the concerns of the person at the end of this chain. Consider this person carefully. She may be the one you have to reach if you really want action.

M.O.D. #2: Chronology

When you need to summarize the history of a product or situation stressing its relationship to time, use a chronological M.O.D. Accident reports and progress reports are typically arranged in time order. The data of each event or change will structure your plan. If you use this method, beware of getting too involved in detail. Stick to major, consequential facts. Your goal is to provide a quick, easy-to-follow review or plan.

Chronological development presents two major problems. First, the time order may force important material to appear in an unemphatic position—such as the middle. Unimportant issues may get unwarranted emphasis by appearing at the beginning and end. In this case, state the most important idea or recommendation at the beginning, ignoring time association. Then shift to chronological development. It saves the hurried reader time digging out pertinent information.

Second, chronological order can be monotonous. Don't begin each sentence with a date. Vary your sentences by putting time words like "then" or "next" in different places. This is guaranteed to be more appealing to your reader.

USEFUL FOR: Processes, growth statistics, accident reports, trip results, test results, progress reports, manufacturing and scientific procedures, journals, minutes of meetings, planning reports, audit reports, test protocols.

M.O.D. #3: Process

To use the Process M.O.D., present your material as if you were writing instructions or a recipe. Each step may be as important as the next. Process differs from chronology in that you need not necessarily mention *when* the actions must take place, only that they must occur in a particular order. Make sure you really understand the task you are describing so that your points will appear in the correct place. This M.O.D. is useful for explaining a chemical process or how to operate, install, or repair a piece of machinery.

USEFUL FOR: Instructions, descriptions of processes, handbooks, user manuals, procedures, training materials.

M.O.D. #4: Organization in Space

Organize your writing spatially when you're dealing with different locations. You may be reporting statistics geographically in a sales report that starts on the East Coast and moves across the country to the West Coast, or by your company's sales-office locations. Spatial order doesn't have to be on a grand scale. You can use it to describe detail on your new office computer from left to right, top to bottom, or exterior to interior.

With this M.O.D., you can create a coherent and concrete order that's easy to follow. It's like connecting the dots in a child's dot-to-dot book. You're given the dots—can you connect them in a way that creates a very clear picture? (Unlike in a dot-to-dot book, there may be more than one good structure that works.) As you lead your readers from place to place, you create a visual image for them—it's like giving them a map.

One warning: Spatial organization in long reports can be just as monotonous as the chronological method. Make a conscious effort to vary sentences and substitute new phrases for overused ones. Try not to be mechanical.

USEFUL FOR: Development or trip reports, descriptions of machinery, building sites, inventions, sales research reports (by specific company division, district, East-West, United States–overseas).

M.O.D. #5: Comparison/Contrast

Comparison is a technique for juxtaposing things to emphasize their similarities; contrast emphasizes differences. This M.O.D. is also useful for discussing advantages and disadvantages.

For example, you may be asked to study and evaluate two possible sites for your new downtown office. If there are more advantages than disadvantages, first present all the advantages of both sites. Then present the disadvantages of the two sites.

Avoid mixing statements about advantages and disadvantages in the same section. This confuses readers. Arrange your comparison this way:

1. Advantages—Site A and Site B
2. Disadvantages—Site A and Site B

Instead of this way:

1. Site A—advantages and disadvantages
2. Site B—advantages and disadvantages

Be coherent in your comparisons by using key phrases, such as:

• on one hand	• the latter	• in the same way	• in opposition to this
• on the other hand	• in this way	• on the contrary	• although that is true
• the former	• in contrast	• but then	

Comparisons are valuable for explaining the unfamiliar to your reader by relating it to the familiar. When comparing two subjects, always mention the more familiar one first. This is the best way to help the reader to understand the lesser-known subject. For example, if you were trying to explain an airplane to someone who'd never seen one, you'd start by comparing it to a bird. Alien ideas have often been understood by comparison: the Indians called the first trains "iron horses."

Beware of comparing too much technical information in writing if graphs or charts would be more helpful.

USEFUL FOR: Feasibility studies, research results, planning reports, some proposals.

M.O.D. #6: Specific to General or General to Specific

This M.O.D. helps you inform, instruct, or persuade your reader. If your challenge is to present a general idea and the specifics (or examples) that describe it, which should come first? This depends on whether or not your reader is already acquainted with the subject matter.

For example, what if you had to explain a camera to a caveman? He probably wouldn't show a jot of interest in the little black box unless you first presented the specifics: a neat snapshot of his bludgeon, a record of his greatest hunting feats, the excitement of instant development and—most remarkable—a picture of himself. You would be leading him to understanding from specifics to the general idea: camera.

On the other hand, what if you were explaining the latest high-tech camera to an expert photographer? Obviously, you'd start by mentioning the camera and then proceed to describe its fantastic features. The photographer is already familiar with the concept of a camera, so it makes sense to open with it. You're reminding him of something familiar to orient him to the subsequent new information about the camera's special options.

If you're deciding whether to present specifics or generality first and your goal is to persuade, reread Mary Kennedy's reasons-opinion decision in M.O.D. #1, Order of Importance. The principle is the same. Consider the specifics to be your reasons and the generality, your opinion.

USEFUL FOR: Proposals, feasibility reports, work orders, training materials, letters of understanding, customer service letters.

M.O.D. #7: Analysis

Use an analytic M.O.D. to interpret the how and why of a situation by taking it apart. Your mechanic uses the same process when he disassembles your car's engine to find out what's wrong. This format is a logical one for analyzing data you've collected. Description of parts will lead to a clear overall assessment.

Imagine you're writing an evaluation for a venture capitalist, Mr. Terry Z., who is trying to decide whether to invest everything he has in the latest high-tech mousetrap. You have a twenty-page report documenting the research and development of the mousetrap.

How should you analyze the report to help Mr. Z. decide? Examine each factor that contributed to the results of the study. Weigh each carefully—one or two factors are bound to emerge as significant.

Analytical development requires a sharp, detail-minded writer. You can't overlook a single aspect with this M.O.D.: the potential market, the people behind the product, the projected mouse population for the next decade, costs, competition, manufacturing plans—everything. You're searching for the critical factors that will mean success. Or failure.

As with all other M.O.D.'s, be conscious of your reader. Often companies use the analytical method for company-growth reports intended for the public. Simplify in-company technical language to ensure easy readability.

USEFUL FOR: Technical reports, yearly overviews, analyses of trends, annual reports, demographic studies, economic forecasts, financial analyses.

Other factors in your choice of M.O.D.

Determining your readers' needs is not the only criterion for choosing your Method of Development. You will discover that certain types of information just naturally lend themselves to a particular method. For example, how could you fail to choose a chronological M.O.D. if your report were entitled "From Minitrix, Inc., 1979, to Megatrix, Inc., 1999: How the Company Grew"?

As you can see, many of the M.O.D.'s explained in this chapter resemble one another. Combine as many as you need to create the structure that presents your material most clearly and, if necessary, persuasively.

ON YOUR OWN: Read over some old reports written by you or your colleagues to see if you can detect what M.O.D.'s they used. Label the different types in the margin. Was one method favored over others?

HOW TO ORGANIZE REPORTS

Practice exercise: try organizing a typical management report

The situation: you have created an outline for a report you're writing. Now you must arrange the segments in the most persuasive and logical sequence. Number the segments below in the best order.

___ Analysis & Supporting Data	___ Executive Summary
___ Purpose of Report	___ Background
___ Appendices	___ Recommendations
___ Title Page	___ Final Summary

Let's compare your answers with ours

We're sure you started with the Title Page, as we did. The big issue is what comes next. We chose the Executive Summary. This section—sometimes called "Management Overview," "Preliminary Summary," or "Abstract"—should always precede the body of the report.

Why begin with an Executive Summary?

Although this summary can be the key to a successful report, many writers neglect it or hesitate to use it. It is, however, essential that any document of three pages or more contain a short, informative overview. Once readers have read the executive summary, they can skim the entire report, get to the main point quickly, and concentrate on only those facts that are important to them.

How long should the Executive Summary be?

The key words are *short* and *informative.* Obviously, it would be a waste of time for both you and your readers if you wrote your report twice—once as a summary, once as the real thing. Depending on the nature of your material, the section should briefly present your purpose and recommendations. In audit reports, for example, a sentence or two describing the scope is appropriate.

What follows the Executive Summary?

Here is one way of sequencing the full report:

1	Title Page	5	Analysis & Supporting Data
2	Executive Summary	6	Background
3	Purpose of Report	7	Final Summary
4	Recommendations	8	Appendices

Why this approach?

Since the function of your report is to present recommendations, hiding them at the end would be counterproductive. As soon as you give the important details about your purpose, state the recommendations.

Near your recommendations include "convincers" to support your point of view. Your readers are busy people: if you don't persuade them in the first few pages, they may not give you a second chance. Many managers tell us that they often read only the first few pages of a report.

Six Steps to Reader-Centered Writing

Now you can present your analysis and background. They are often inter-changeable. Are you surprised that "Background" appears so late in the report? Often writers give too much attention to background information. Whenever you present it, ask yourself if it's really vital to the readers' understanding. If you're just recapping a bit of history your readers already know, move it toward the end, into the appendix, or perhaps eliminate it altogether.

Concluding your report

The Final Summary contains another reminder of your major goal and persuaders. It's your last chance to convince your readers. Use it! At the back of the report, include appendices, if necessary. These should contain important information that does not belong in the body of the report, such as facts that most readers may know, but one or two may not.

SEQUENCE WITH A WORD PROCESSOR

As we discussed in Step 3, the greatest benefit of word processing is the ease of moving text. You can instantly move words, sentences, paragraphs, entire pages. You'll find instructions on moving text in your user's manual or in one of the "help menus" included in your word-processing program.

Word processing makes sequencing very easy. Try one order of ideas. If you'd like to try a different order, you can rearrange the material with a few simple commands. Even moments before you make a final printout for distribution (or just before you press "send" on the electronic mail system), you still have one more chance to evaluate the order of your ideas for impact. Just remember to change your transitions accordingly. (See Step 5 for more on transitions.)

HOW DO YOU ORGANIZE YOUR WRITING TIME?

By now I fear you may be thinking, *If I do all the planning you're suggesting, it's going to take me twice as long to write, not half as long.* Fortunately, this isn't true, and the proof is in the following chart.

Fill in the left-hand columns. To write a typical memo, what percentage of your time do you spend in each category? Now look at the second column. This is how professional writers allocate their time. If you follow our Six Steps, you too will find yourself dividing your time this way. The result? You'll join the ranks of the thousands of our graduates who say that they've cut one third off their writing time.

Are You Organizing Your Writing Time the Way Professional Writers Do?

Your Time	Professional Writers	
_____ %	_50%_	Plan
_____ %	_20%_	Draft
_____ %	_30%_	Edit

You have just finished the planning stage of the writing process. All your hard work is about to pay off as you zoom through your first draft.

STEP FIVE
Write the First Draft

Using your plan

Now that you've clustered and sequenced your ideas, you are ready to write a quick-and-dirty first draft. The challenge is to write only—without editing. Don't let the critic in you compete with your creative self as you draft sentences! Wait until all your ideas are on paper before polishing and refining your writing. Editing each sentence as you write it only breaks your concentration.

Content versus form

After the planning stages, the writing task consists of two very different activities: (1) generating content—a creative process; (2) structuring the form—an analytic process. If you try to do both activities at the same time, you will lose your speed. For example, if in the middle of the first draft, you stop for five minutes to grope for the perfect word, you'll no doubt grind to a halt. Leave a space where the word belongs and fill it in later. Try to keep up your speed as you did when free writing.

Start anywhere

Don't get hung up on that first, most difficult sentence. You can sit at your desk for hours—if you've got nothing better to do—worriedly rewriting your opener. If the first sentence is not immediately apparent, forget about it and get on with your writing. You can go back later, when the pressure is off, and put in the missing sentence. Some of the best beginnings are written last—after you totally understand your intentions.

Headlines help you decide where to start

Review the headlines you created in Step 3 to decide which sections you'll tackle first. Maybe you're the type who prefers to get the easy material out of the way immediately. On the other hand, you may want to go after a difficult section first because you feel alert and up to the challenge. In short, start with whatever section appeals to you.

HOW TO CONSTRUCT PARAGRAPHS

Before you launch into your first draft, it's worth reviewing paragraph construction. Paragraphs are the *meat and potatoes* of any document. They have three purposes:
- to develop the single idea presented in the topic sentence or headline
- to provide a logical break in material
- to create physical breaks that help the reader visually

Well-constructed paragraphs have unity and coherence. Unity means focusing on one idea. Coherence means linking sentences and ideas with transitional words.

Stick to one idea for each paragraph (for unity)

When you ramble from idea to idea, you lose your readers' attention. Most readers prefer to handle one idea at a time. They count on paragraph breaks to signal the completion of one topic and the beginning of the next.

Begin with a topic sentence or headline. Since your readers usually want to get the point immediately, present a summary of your paragraph's main point early. The Bottom-Line-on-Top principle applies to paragraphs, too. Here are some examples of effective topic sentences:
- Capital spending declined drastically in April.
- The XYZ System will reduce overhead by 50%.
- Ginnie Maes can provide worry-free investment income.

In each case, the writer needs to explain more to complete the paragraph, but must hold back information that doesn't relate to the topic sentence.

Incorporate transitions and connectors for coherence

Transition words such as *therefore* and *however* are signposts that help your readers follow your logic, your flow of ideas. Be careful to choose the appropriate transition. The sentences that follow show how meaning changes with different transition words, and how unclear the point remains if no transitions are used.

1. Jessica is compiling the research. I'll interview the client.
2. Jessica is compiling the research. Meanwhile, I'll interview the client.
3. Jessica is compiling the research. However, I'll interview the client.
4. Jessica is compiling the research. Therefore, I'll interview the client.

Do your readers a favor: use transitions to link your ideas both between or within sentences and between paragraphs.

How to use transition words

Choose your transition words according to the relationship you want to establish between ideas. Here are some examples:

CONTRAST
however, although, but, conversely, nevertheless, yet, still, on the other hand

COMPARISON
similarly, likewise, in the same way

CAUSE AND EFFECT
as a result, therefore, consequently, thus, so, because

EXAMPLE
for instance, for example, specifically, as an illustration

ADDITION
moreover, besides, in addition, also, too

TIME
now, later, after, before, meanwhile, following, then

SEQUENCE
first, second, third, next, last, finally

Incorporate conjunctions as transitional connectors

The coordinating conjunctions—*and, but, yet, or, nor, for*—are used to connect ideas *within* sentences. They also can be used like the transition words listed above—that is, to connect ideas *between* sentences—although traditional grammarians may object in some cases.

Traditionalists say you can't start a sentence with one of these conjunctions. However, other writing experts suggest that occasional use of a coordinating conjunction to begin a sentence improves the flow and clarity of a paragraph. And we agree.

Carefully choose a coordinating conjunction to show *precisely* the relationship of ideas you intend. For example, use *and* only to show that the next idea is an *addition* to the previous idea.

Beware: • Don't use *and* when *but* is more precise.
             • Don't use *and* merely to string ideas together.

Use reference words and repetition for linkage

Link your ideas by referring to or repeating the topic or key words. Use reference words like *this, that, these, those,* and other pronouns to tie in new ideas with points made earlier. Within and between paragraphs, linkage gives logical flow to your thoughts.

Paragraphs are the building blocks

Now that we've reviewed how to write an effective paragraph and the uses of transitions and connectors, it's time to start writing.

WRITE THE FIRST DRAFT

Write down a headline, then write a paragraph

Without regard to style or grammar, write one paragraph for each headline. Be bold—put down your thoughts, even if the sentences are messy and graceless. Resist your internal critic if it tries to derail your train of thought. You can clean up the draft later.

Add more headlines as subtopics emerge

Don't be surprised if you haven't thought in advance of every possible headline you'll need in your document. As you write, you'll no doubt discover many sub-ideas you need to mention. Simply add headlines or topic sentences as you need them—this is a predictable part of the process.

The myth of the perfect first draft

No matter what they say on the talk shows, very few professional writers produce a perfect draft the first time around. F. Scott Fitzgerald's stories went through a minimum of five drafts before publication. Even after an experienced writer has worked on a manuscript, it goes to a professional editor for revision and polishing before it goes to press.

People who believe it's possible to write a perfect draft the first time around probably think that's the most efficient way to write. Unfortunately, this misconception prevents them from using their time well. In fact, writers who aim to produce a perfect document with their first draft usually find themselves facing paralysis and confusion. This is because they are trying to do two very different things at once: write and edit.

To save time and minimize frustration, simply dive into this first draft with the aim of getting *something* on paper, rather than trying to get it perfect. For hints on drafting with a word processor, see the facing page.

Efficiency tip: try writing with a time limit

One way to start your first draft is to write with a time limit. The ticking clock may prevent you from daydreaming. As in the Free-Writing approach, fill a page as quickly as you can, but this time, do not allow your thoughts to wander. Stick to the ideas you've clustered under each headline. (If you find the time pressure bringing on writer's block, this strategy is not for you.)

❧ ON YOUR OWN: Try drafting a paragraph.

Time yourself as you draft a paragraph on "What We Can Do to Improve Our Department," or on any other topic of your choice. Write your start time at the top of the page. Then, when you're finished, write your finish time at the bottom of the page.

How long did it take you? If you filled the page in five minutes or under, you're doing well. If it took you longer than five minutes, or if you filled only half a page, you were probably worrying too much about word choice or sentence construction. It's the myth of the perfect first draft again! You should be able to write down several ideas quickly, even if they are roughly worded.

Try the exercise once more on another topic, and *don't* edit yourself as you go along.

DRAFT WITH A WORD PROCESSOR

With your headlines chosen and sequenced, you can begin to write a draft on your word processor. One workshop participant called it "exploding the outline." Here's how it works. Turn on your computer and open the "headlines" file for your document. Begin with any headline—the topic you feel most comfortable with—and write a paragraph under it. Then, move on to each subsequent headline until you've finished your entire draft.

Adding new headlines and paragraphs as you go or inserting them later will be easier on a computer because you won't have to use a new piece of paper or retype earlier paragraphs. When you're finished drafting, print out your document to see how it looks on paper.

TRY DICTATING YOUR FIRST DRAFT

Many seasoned writers find that the first draft flows more easily from their lips than from their fingertips. Those with experience estimate that they can dictate about six times faster than they can write. If you could increase your productivity by six times, wouldn't it be worth switching to this method?

In Step 5, don't brainstorm, follow your plan

When we covered dictating in Step 2, we explained how to move random, unorganized ideas from your brain onto the page. Unlike in Step 2, when you rarely turned off the "record" button, during Step 5 dictate your draft allowing yourself the luxury of pausing. When you need a minute to regroup or formulate a thought, turn off the "record" button.

To begin

First, check the equipment to make sure the sound is clear and loud enough for your transcriber or typist to hear. Then, keeping your sequenced Start-up Strategy or notes before you, begin drafting your document by saying the sentences, rather than writing them down. Even if you feel a little awkward at first, keep going.

Remember, you're dictating a first draft

Don't worry about perfection. Avoid editing or censoring the words you speak—just as you would avoid editing if you were *writing* the draft for Step 5. For now, you just want to get the draft on tape; you can correct your grammar and sentence structure when the draft comes back on paper.

Dictated drafts need careful editing

Avoid the common error of mailing out your unedited draft. To convince you, here is the dictated draft of the next paragraph:

> Dictated drafts have a stream-of-consciousness quality. You say whatever words come to mind. The words might not be as clear at first. In other words, you probably say more words the first time you try to express the thought than you'd really need to use if you thought about it more. That's what editing can do for you—editing gives you a chance to boil down your words and ideas—to crystallize them into their simplest form. But I don't want to talk about editing too much, because we'll cover that in Step 6. For now, just make sure you don't think you're finished once you've dictated all the ideas and had the typist prepare a transcript.

Is the above as clear and concise as it could have been? No. We repeated the same point several times, and didn't vary sentence construction enough. We also repeated several words and phrases unnecessarily. Use dictating to get your paragraphs written, but always review the transcript carefully. Some good news: you've saved so much time by dictating that you'll come out ahead, even after editing.

Is it time to edit yet?

If you've managed to avoid editing yourself until now, you should feel proud. It's not easy to keep writing while your internal critic is giving you a running commentary on your every word. Before you pick up your red pencil to edit, there's one more step to help you shift gears.

GET DISTANCE

What is getting distance?

If you're too close to your work, it's hard to be objective about it. Getting distance means putting your writing away for a while so that you can come back to it with a fresh perspective. With enough time between writing and reviewing, it will be easier to approach your material as if someone else had written it. Other people's errors are easier to spot than your own.

For example, you may think you wrote perfectly clear instructions for your assistant to purchase a new workstation. When you review your memo, you realize you forgot to specify the type of financing you wanted him to arrange—a potentially costly omission.

Another example is the following ad. Can you find the ambiguity?

Was the advertiser an employer who wanted to hire a typist, or a typist who was looking for a job? It's impossible to tell. The newspaper insertion was a waste of both time and money.

How much time can you spare?

Of course, it's often difficult to allow yourself the luxury of getting distance with your schedule filled with do-it-now deadlines. However, getting distance is *an integral part of the editing process.* If putting your writing away for a day or two is impossible, then try to plan to complete your first draft just before you leave for the day. Even a lunch break or a ten-minute walk will help. You owe it to yourself and your reader to leave time between the writing and the editing.

STEP SIX
Edit for Clarity, Conciseness, and Accuracy

Welcome back from your "getting distance" trip. You've arrived at Step 6, and it's time to edit. From this vantage point, you will be able to revise so that your reader can understand you quickly and easily. This section focuses on the basics of editing—not grammar. For a grammar review, turn to page 131.

USE THE "BE YOUR OWN EDITOR" CHECKLIST

The "Be Your Own Editor" Checklist that follows serves as an outline for this chapter. More important, it will become the checklist you use from now on to make sure your document is reader-centered. The Checklist reminds you to refine and polish the draft, then guides you through the remaining steps—right up to your final signature.

Now let's look more closely at each phase in the editing process—beginning with a quick review of Steps 1–4.

Review Steps 1–4

Before you go any further, stop to review what you have done. Then you'll be ready to put your document in final form. There's no point in refining and polishing your draft until you're sure you've followed the writing process.

The "Be Your Own Editor" Checklist

CONTENT

Information: ☐ Accurate and complete?
                     ☐ Right amount of details?
                     ☐ Benefits included in persuasive documents?
Purpose: ☐ Stated clearly?
                     ☐ Specific requests for action or information?

SEQUENCE

Bottom Line: ☐ At the top?
                     ☐ Strategically placed?
Organization: ☐ Do ideas flow logically?

DESIGN

Format: ☐ Enough headlines, sidelines, and lists?
                     ☐ White space to frame ideas?
                     ☐ Deadlines and action items highlighted?
Presentation: ☐ Would a chart, table, or graph be more effective for certain information?

STRUCTURE

Paragraphs: ☐ Begin with a topic sentence?
                     ☐ Focused on one topic?
                     ☐ Transitions within and between?
                     ☐ Limited to 5–6 lines?
Sentences: ☐ Varied in structure and length?
                     ☐ Streamlined to 15–20 words?

continued

The "Be Your Own Editor" Checklist, *continued*

TONE/STYLE

Words: ☐ Simple, specific, and straightforward?
☐ Free of affectation and gobbledygook?
☐ Acronyms explained?
☐ Terminology familiar to readers?
☐ Headlines worded for impact?

Style: ☐ Personable, upbeat, and direct?
☐ Appropriate for the audience?
☐ Active voice?
☐ Positive approach?

PROOFREAD

☐ Grammar, spelling, and punctuation accurate?
☐ Typographical errors corrected?
☐ Should someone else review it?
☐ If this is a repeat mailing, is new data highlighted?

Add your personal bugaboos
to complete the checklist.

☐ _____
☐ _____
☐ _____
☐ _____
☐ _____
☐ _____

Review Step 1: Analyze your purpose and audience

This review is essential if you are to do an effective editing job. By reviewing your analysis, you will have it fresh in your mind. Use this review to refocus on your audience and purpose. If you discover you've changed your mind about either, you must redo (not review) Steps 1–4.

Review Step 2: Generate ideas

With your audience and purpose in mind, see if you have included the right information as well as the right *amount* of information. Knowing exactly how much information to present isn't always easy. It takes as much skill to decide what to omit as what to include. Ask yourself:
- Do I have enough data to inform or persuade my reader?
- Am I including too much?
- What is necessary and relevant for my audience and purpose?

It's not too late to add or delete ideas, but remember: less is more. Make your writing as brief as possible.

Review Step 3: Group information under headlines

Again, with audience and purpose in mind, check the headlines you've written for each paragraph. Are they on target? Do they truly describe the contents of the paragraph? Are paragraphs short and well constructed? Do they each contain just one idea? Do they use enough transitions and connectors to make good sense and smooth reading?

Review Step 4: Sequence your ideas

Have you chosen the most useful method of development to suit both your audience and purpose? Have you organized your report so that your readers don't have to go through the process of discovery (as you did when you researched the report)? For example, are meeting minutes organized chronologically while giving emphasis to significant developments or decisions?

This is your last chance to change the sequence of information if you think of a more effective one. Is your "bottom line" on top? Or as close as possible?

Are you satisfied with what you have so far?

If your answer is yes, then think about your document's visual impact. You're ready to proceed to the next step in the editing process: designing your document to best present your message.

If your answer is no, try the following technique:

The rewriting strategy

Sometimes your letter or memo (or paragraph) just doesn't sound right. In this situation, it may be more efficient simply to put away your draft and start again.

Words are not precious; there are plenty more where the first ones came from. The Nobel Prize–winning writer Isaac Bashevis Singer calls the wastebasket "the writer's best friend."

∞ ON YOUR OWN: Quickly write a one-page memo on any topic. After you've finished, fold it up and start again. Don't look at the first one. Repeat the process a second time. Now compare the three drafts. Chances are you'll prefer a later draft. Why?

Suggested topic:
You recently interviewed Mr. Paul Tree for an important position in your department. You think he'd be great for the job, but you've heard he's about to take a position elsewhere. In a letter, offer him the position and try to convince him that this is his best choice.

This rewriting strategy is designed to prove that rewriting can be as efficient as revising when you're stuck. Take the strategy seriously. For some frustrated managers, rewriting has dramatically changed their ability to get past the tough spots. Professional writers use it constantly. Try it enough times to give it a chance to work.

Design for Visual Impact

What is visual impact?

When a document is easy to read and key points seem to jump out at you—that document has visual impact. Clear writing alone is not enough. Take the time to create a visual design that *entices* readers. Visual design will help your message stand out from the hundreds of documents that regularly bombard readers.

Put yourself in your readers' shoes

When you check through the material in your in-box, what makes you read one document instead of another? Without even realizing it, you probably choose documents that look appealing because they:
- use headlines liberally
- keep paragraphs short
- include lists
- allow for plenty of white space
- underscore important steps or dates
- use a different typeface to make important information stand out.

Making your format work for you

Consciously or unconsciously, readers develop attitudes toward a piece of writ-

HOW TO DESIGN FOR VISUAL IMPACT

USE   **HEADLINES**
for almost every paragraph
to focus your reader on major ideas

SIDELINES
for extra emphasis
for persuasion

SHORT PARAGRAPHS (5–6 lines)
to avoid overwhelming your reader
to attract speed readers

BULLETED LISTS
to replace lists within sentences

NUMBERED LISTS
when sequence is important
when listing steps in a procedure
for ease in referring to the list later

WHITE SPACE AND INDENTATION
to frame your ideas
to improve readability

GRAPHS, CHARTS, OR TABLES
to present numbers, dates, dollars, or data

HIGHLIGHT   *Deadlines and Action Items*
with:

> <u>Underlining</u>
> **Boldface Type**
> ALL CAPITALS
> *Italics*
> Different Fonts
> Different Size Types

ing—and the writer—from the appearance of the writing alone. They make judgments about how difficult it is to read or how organized it may be. Readers notice and appreciate a writer's effort when a document is visually appealing. Carefully designed documents tell your readers that you care not only about your message but about them. Make your format work *for* you—not against you.

The "How to Design for Visual Impact" checklist

Even the simplest formatting techniques make a big difference in the appearance and the readability of your document. Now that you've finished your draft, design your document using the checklist. Use it to review all of your writing until it becomes second nature.

Let's examine each of the formatting techniques on the checklist. Don't think that designing is just busywork; the more visual impact your document has, the more likely that someone will give it prompt attention.

Use headlines for most paragraphs in reports and memos

As we discussed in Step 3, headlining means choosing a few words that illustrate the content of the paragraph, underlining them, and introducing each paragraph with them. The appearance of the headline (placement, underscoring, special type) signals your readers. It tells them where to look for key ideas and promises them easy reading.

Use sidelines for extra emphasis and persuasion

Like headlines and "RE:" lines, sidelines attract readers' attention and may add to a document's persuasiveness. Sidelines are functionally the same as headlines; it's just that they are placed to the left side of the text. In the boxed example that follows, the sidelines are use, underline, and consider.

Use:	• Headlines
	• Sidelines
	• Bullets
Underline:	• Action Steps
Consider:	• Typeface Options

The following is a good example of sidelines in a proposal.

Tuition Reimbursement Proposal

HOW THIS PLAN WILL FURTHER CORPORATE GOALS

Controls Attrition	The service contract will insure that Glitch, Inc. gets a return from its investments in employee graduate education.
Controls Costs	Only employees who continue in service to Glitch will have courses or degrees paid for by Glitch funds.
	Other companies have experienced a decline in cost when they added a service requirement. We cannot, however, guarantee Glitch will experience a similar decline.
Supports Affirmative Action	Women and minorities will have the opportunity to fight "credentialism" by earning the advanced degrees that are perceived as necessary for upward mobility. The Legal Department supports this approach.
Encourages Productivity and Motivation	The "new breed" of workers—young, educated, and ambitious—expects developmental and educational options. The new policy will encourage greater productivity in two ways: improved educational options will help motivate employees while the education programs will improve their business and professional skills.
Improves Recruitment and Retention	This policy will enable Glitch to meet the competition in recruiting and retaining high-quality employees. The proposed policy will give line managers more developmental and motivational tools.

Notice the visual impact of different type styles and sizes in this excerpt from a technical document.

Conversion Doc. 17

On-Line Table Handling

Two Types of Tables

A table can be internal to the programs which use it or can be kept external and loaded when needed.

A. Internal Tables

How to access COBOL copy statement
An internal table is included with the programs which use it in one of two ways. First, it can be copied into the program using a COBOL copy statement. To test a new version of such tables requires a recompilation and relink edit of all the programs which use it.

Link editing
Second, a table can be link edited with a program. To access the table, the COBOL program calls the routine containing the table to pass it back to the calling program. A change to such a table causes a relink edit of all the programs which use it to include the new copy.

Overhead
Although a change to an internal table causes some action to be taken on each program which uses it, little or no overhead is involved in accessing it.

B. External Tables

How to access
External tables are accessed by the COBOL program by calling an assembler language routine which loads the table from an external library and passes it back to the calling program.

C. Batch

Table source
In a batch environment, the first time a request is made by the program for an external table, the table is obtained from the available copy previously loaded. When the program terminates, the table is automatically deleted by IMS/VS.

Keep paragraphs to 5–6 typed lines maximum

A paragraph can be just one sentence or several. It is best, though, for visual impact, to package ideas in neat paragraphs of five to six typed lines consisting of several sentences. Long paragraphs look difficult to the reader. Find a place to break them up.

Also, make paragraphs short to keep the attention of speed readers. Those trained in speed reading often read only the first line of every paragraph. The more paragraphs you make, the more they'll read.

An occasional one-sentence paragraph can be emphatic when you want a single idea to jump out at the reader, but a two-, three-, or four-sentence paragraph is the norm. Most often, you will need several sub-ideas to explain or expand the key idea. In any case, it's not just the paragraph length that has visual impact—it's the white space created between paragraphs that makes for easy reading. (This was a three-sentence paragraph.)

Use bullets or hyphens for each item in a list

Bullets are the little solid black circles (•) that you frequently see to the left of items in a list. (To create a bullet, type a lower-case *o* and blacken it in. Put two spaces between a bullet and the paragraph or line.) You may also use hyphens (-) and asterisks (*) this way. These marks attract the reader's attention and make a list easy to digest.

Use numbers to emphasize sequence, for steps in a procedure, or for later reference

When you want to show that the items in your list have a certain priority or order, use numbers instead of bullets or hyphens. Numbers are especially helpful when you are explaining "how to." They provide a visual signal that tells the reader how to read the information and an easy reference mechanism for discussing documents with others.

Use white space to frame your ideas

White space is created by separating paragraphs and sections. It also occurs between headlines and text and in the margins—top, bottom, left, and right. White space gives the reader a visual break—relief from the dense look of text. Moreover, white space surrounding text showcases important information.

Use indentation to highlight sub-ideas or lists

Traditionally, we think of indenting as a way to introduce a new paragraph. This type of indenting is going out of fashion with the popularity of the word processor, which "wraps" words. Readers already know a new idea is starting because of the space between paragraphs.

By contrast, indenting sub-ideas within a paragraph will call your reader's attention to the big picture. Indent to send a visual signal to your reader that you are supporting a key idea with data that explains or expands it. The white space created by the indentation draws the reader's eye to the list and makes for easy reference later.

Underline action items for the reader

Underlining calls attention to key action steps, dates, deadlines. Our trainers use the motto "Deadlines demand headlines." In addition, you can use underlining to highlight vital words, phrases, or ideas. Caution: Don't overdo underlining; it will lose its impact.

Do you send revised versions or updates?

Many times you learn just after mailing a document that a detail has changed. Perhaps:

- the deadline has been moved up or back
- a new workshop will be added
- a final product decision was announced

Alert your readers to changes by:

- sending a new memo noting only the change, or
- updating your original memo and marking the change with a highlighter

One executive told me his biggest pet peeve was "having to reread the whole document to sleuth out what was different from the first version."

Do you have typeface options?

Word processors and many typewriters offer typeface options, for example, **bold**, *italics,* ALL CAPITALS. These can draw attention to a word, phrase, or sentence. But like too much underlining, using too many typefaces can spoil the effect. Don't overdo it.

If you have a word processor, you can choose from countless type styles and font sizes, too. The possibilities for visual design are virtually limitless with the advent of desktop publishing. Find out what is available to you and experiment. Again, beware of "too much of a good thing."

Consider using graphics

One picture truly can be worth a thousand words, as the old saw goes. Where appropriate, try using graphics to draw attention to your document. A manager I once knew photocopied newspaper cartoons on many of his memos to get the attention of his salespeople. Others have used little drawings to add visual appeal.

Certain desktop publishing packages allow you to create drawings and incorporate them into your documents. Others offer ready-made artwork. If you haven't used such software yet, you're in for a treat.

Consider using charts, graphs, and tables

Charts, graphs, and tables allow you to present information in a more visually appealing way than by using straight text. It's often easier for readers to grasp information when it is presented graphically, rather than in words.

Software packages are available for creating eye-opening graphs, charts, and tables. Desktop publishing not only makes it easy to create these visuals but produces professional-looking results. Writers without state-of-the-art equipment should use traditional methods to compete visually.

Consider using attachments

Attachments are a visually (and intellectually) appealing way to include supplementary information. By including attachments at the end of the document, you avoid interrupting the flow of ideas.

Longer or more detailed charts, tables, and graphs may be better placed in an attachment. You will have to decide whether the space they take up merits placing them within the text. You will also have to decide whether placing them there helps or distracts readers.

Other information—background, explanation, illustration—also can be placed in attachments. When referred to an attachment, readers can readily find and read the information when, and if, they wish.

Are you satisfied with the visual design?

If you are, then you are finished formatting your first draft. Now it's time to take another look at your headlines. Are they as *reader-centered* as possible?

Rewrite Headlines: Add Impact

If the headlines used in your draft were drawn primarily from the list of *generic* headlines on pages 32 and 33, then your headlines may lack the pizazz needed to entice the reader. Don't worry. Great headlines are rarely apparent the first time around. Like other aspects of the reader-centered writing process, headline writing gets easier with practice.

How to catch the reader's attention

First, scan your headlines. Do they flow in a logical sequence? Do they lead readers in the direction you want? Good headlines provide the reader with a quick overview of the document's major issues and follow a strategic method of development.

Next, ask yourself these questions:
- Are my headlines specific and accurate?
- Do they direct readers to my key points?
- Is action emphasized?

- Are they worded positively? Are they direct, yet polite?
- Do they reach out to my readers?
- Do action items and deadlines stand out?

If your headlines could be better, here are some remedies for refining headlines so they have maximum effect.

From boring to bold

Write a better headline without missing your deadline. Take one of these extra strength remedies:

Remedy #1: Be Specific   Replace a too broad and boring headline with a more concrete term—or combine the two.

Boring: "Background"
Better: "Digitcorp and the microchip revolution"

Boring: "Rationale"
Better: "Rationale: to avoid potential liability"

Remedy #2: Include your Point   This is B.L.O.T. (Bottom Line on Top) at its best!

Boring: "Recommendations"
Better: "Recommendation: improve employee training"

Boring: "Overview of our divestiture policy"
Better: "How divestiture has improved our balance sheet"

Remedy #3: Emphasize Action   Highlight action by using active verbs.

Boring: "Step one"
Better: "Getting started: reach for that Focus Sheet"

Boring: "Last step"
Better: "Be your own editor and wrap it up right"

Boring: "Implementation"
Better: "Action recommended: test Equilab method in a pilot project"

Boring: "Background"
Better: "Why Cliptronics undertook an absenteeism study" or "What started it all" or "How employee involvement brought about this project"

Remedy #4: Be Positive   Good news attracts *and* persuades.

Negative: "Problem: absenteeism in the workplace"
Better: "Opportunity: increase productivity by reducing absenteeism"

Remedy #5: Ask Questions   You'll find that they:
- combine the best of the above techniques
- are often part of your Start-Up strategy
- appeal to your *readers'* issues

Boring: "R.O.I."
Better: "What will be our Return on Investment (R.O.I.)?"

Boring: "Meeting agenda items"
Better: "What should this meeting accomplish?"

Boring: "Ordering procedure"
Better: "How can you take advantage of this special price?"

Boring: "Timetable"
Better: "When can you expect the results?"

Remedy #6: Remember the "Headlines Hall of Fame"

Use these favorite headlines regularly:

Action requested	Next steps
Action recommended	Deadline
Action required	Action taken
Person to contact	How to . . .

A few final tips from our writers:

1. Brainstorm for words, phrases, or questions that best pinpoint your topic.
2. Try to give more information, rather than less.
3. Be sure to use the active voice.
4. Use a verb whenever you can. "Hire a Staff Accountant" is better than "Staff Accountant."

How creative can I be with my headlines?

Base your decision on an analysis of your audience and the tone you want to create with your words.

"Where there's smoke there's *ire*" was used by a person calling for a no-smoking policy in her office. It worked. But it might not work if smokers and nonsmokers have been at war with one another for years. "How smoke affects nonsmokers' health" might be a better choice in that case.

Edit Paragraphs

Once you're satisfied that your headlines have maximum impact, your next editing challenge is to revise the building blocks of the document—your paragraphs.

How to check your paragraphs

First, scan your paragraphs. Make sure that they are short and that your bottom line is in the first paragraph unless you have deliberately chosen to put it elsewhere. Next, ask yourself these questions:

- Does each of your paragraphs focus on one idea only?
- Does each paragraph begin with a topic sentence or a headline that serves the same purpose?

If not, review the material on paragraph unity, page 58.

- Do the paragraphs flow logically from one to the other?
- Are the ideas within the paragraphs linked with transition words so that their relationships are clear?

If not, review the material on paragraph coherence, page 58.

- Are paragraphs short (five to six lines)?
- Is there is enough white space along all margins?
- Is there adequate spacing between paragraphs?

If not, review the material on making your paragraphs visually appealing, page 68.

Reader-centered paragraphs get results

Revising your paragraphs won't take long if you follow the guidelines described above. The benefit to you is a simple one: you'll increase the chances that your document will be easily understood.

Revise Sentences

Now you're ready to refine and polish sentences. Put yourself in your readers' shoes as you reread each sentence. Use the following techniques to make your sentences straightforward, clear, and direct.

STREAMLINE   Streamlining means weeding out any words or phrases that do not contribute to the readers' understanding. You can eliminate some words or phrases entirely, or eliminate one in a pair of redundant words. For example, replace *at this point in time* with *now* or drop *again* from *resume again.* Hemingway said, "Writing is architecture, not interior decoration." Get rid of the clutter.

Streamlining also means rearranging or dividing sentences. Don't try to put too many ideas in a single sentence. Keep each sentence to one or two ideas. Write other sentences to add new thoughts. Two straightforward, short sentences are easier to follow than a complicated, long one.

Guideline: In general, sentences should be no more than 15 to 20 words each. Longer sentences may be difficult to read easily and to write correctly. They often slow readers down, and may even put them to sleep! On the other hand, sentence length should be varied. A pileup of too many very short sentences will make your writing sound choppy or childish.

Suggestions for streamlining sentences:

- Don't use several words where one will do.
- Don't repeat yourself.
- Use an action verb when possible.
- Avoid *is where* and *is when.*
- Use prepositional phrases sparingly.
- Break long sentences into shorter ones.

Here are some sentences before and after streamlining:

Before: 1. At this point in time, we have not yet decided which action plan we will put into operation.

Revised: 1. We have not yet chosen a plan.

Before: 2. In the event of an unexpected accident and you are a witness who saw the accident, you should file a completed accident report with the office of the safety director.

Revised: 2. If you witness an accident, file an accident report with the safety director.

Before: 3. Managers who are effective give praise to their employees who are outstanding workers and endeavor to implement motivational strategies with subordinates working under them who do not perform well.

Revised: 3. Effective managers praise outstanding employees and try to motivate poor performers.

ON YOUR OWN: To test your skill in streamlining sentences, try the exercises on page 148.

ACTIVATE SENTENCES Make your sentences come alive by using the active voice. Business writers unconsciously overuse the passive voice in sentences like this one: "New procedures will be documented by next month." We are left to guess who is responsible for documenting. The active version is more straightforward and informative: "By next month, the audit department will document the new procedures."

Writing in the passive voice, as the word implies, makes you sound ineffectual. It shows an unwillingness to take responsibility for your actions or to assign responsibility to others. Don't hide behind statements like "Receipt of your letter is acknowledged." Instead, say, "We received your letter" or even "Thank you for your letter." So often we fail to give credit where it is due: "An excellent job was done." By whom?

Need a review?

Let's go over identifying passive voice and changing it to active. Most situations will call for the active voice although both types of sentences are grammatically correct. Passive sentences tend to be ambiguous and wordy. Readers prefer active sentences.

How to recognize active & passive sentences

In the active sentence below the subject plays an active role. The subject performs the action of the verb.

    The manager wrote the report.

The subject (the manager) did perform the action—he did the writing.

In the passive sentences below, the subject plays a passive role. The subject receives the action of the verb and does not perform the action.

    The report was written.

The subject (report) received the action of the verb (writing) in that the report "got written." But the report did not do the writing.

    The report was written by the manager.

The above is *still passive:* the report received the action of writing. Even though in this case we're told who did the writing, "the manager" is not functioning as the subject of the sentence.

    I was authorized to write the report.

The above is passive, too: the subject (I) passively received the authorization and did not *do* the authorizing. (One way to make the sentence active: "John authorized me to write the report.")

Hints for pinpointing passive sentences

- Passive sentences always contain some form of the verb "to be," as a helping verb. The passive sentences highlight this.

Subject (passive recipient)	"to be" verb	
1. Circuit boards	are	inspected daily by John.
2. Research	was	done on the case.
3. Statements	were being	reconciled.
4. Susan	will be	trained on Friday.
5. The checks	have been	sent.
6. Help	is	given to the homeless by XYZ Corporation.
7. I	am	not authorized by the president to approve the checks.

- Sometimes the word "by" appears after the verb (as in examples 6 and 7 above), signaling who does perform the action of the verb.

In summary

You've spotted a passive sentence if the sentence:

1. uses a form of "to be" as a helping verb, *and*
2. the subject of the sentence is not performing the action verb describes

How to activate passive sentences

Once you've identified a passive sentence, follow these three steps to convert your sentence to the active form. To illustrate, let's use this sentence:

`Complaints are taken seriously.`

Step #1 Find or supply the actor: `We`

Step #2 Put the actor (who performs the action) in front of the verb.

`We    are taken`

Step #3 Replace the passive verb with an active form of the verb.

Active Sentence: `We take complaints seriously.`

Practice exercise:

Try activating sentences 1–7 on the previous page using this process. You'll come up with results like these active sentences:

Subject (active actor)	Active verb	
1. John	inspects	circuit boards daily.
2. The manager's staff	did	the research on the case.
3. The department	reconciled	the statements.
4. Eleanor	will train	Susan on Friday.
5. Payroll	has sent	the checks.
6. XYZ Corporation	gives	help to the homeless.
7. The president	has not authorized	me to approve the checks.

Note: Don't confuse passive voice with past tense. Both active and passive sentences can be in any tense. Below are examples of both active and passive sentences written in past, present, and future time.

	Active:	Passive:
Past:	Payroll has sent the checks.	The checks have been sent.
Present:	Payroll is sending the checks.	The checks are being sent.
Future:	Payroll will send the checks.	The checks will be sent.

The passive has its place

The choice of voice is a question of strategy. Sometimes you will want to use the passive voice. For example, if you do not know, or if it doesn't matter, who performed the action, the passive voice will best express your idea.

EXAMPLE: The report was not completed on time. (Your colleague did not complete the report, but you don't want to point a finger at him on paper.)

EXAMPLE: The system was shut down before the data was transferred.

Often it is easier, safer, or more tactful not to say who performed the action in a sentence. The passive voice allows us to express our ideas without naming and blaming anyone.

If the passive voice is useful, why is it frowned upon?

Businesspeople frequently overuse the passive voice because they think it sounds more professional. The passive voice does sound more impersonal, but that is not always desirable; for example: "It has been approved that a promotion to vice-president be given you." This sentence is needlessly cold and awkward.

Use the active voice 90% of the time

Use the passive voice when it isn't desirable to say "who dunnit" or when you want to distance yourself from the message. Otherwise, use the active voice.

ON YOUR OWN: To test your skill in activating sentences, try the exercises in "Quiz Yourself" on page 150.

ELIMINATE GOBBLEDYGOOK   What is it? Gobbledygook is stuffy, pompous language. George Orwell said, "Never use a long word when a short one will do." Long words don't impress educated readers, and they can confuse less-educated ones. Jargon (the special vocabulary of a technical field) and fad words like *reincenti- vize* cloud meaning and slow down readers.

Using gobbledygook doesn't necessarily make you sound more professional; it can make you sound insecure—something no manager can afford. The examples below illustrate the difference between gobbledygook and clear English.

Gobbledygook: We request that you endeavor to locate the communication inasmuch as the manager regards it to be of great importance for today's conference.

Better: Please try to find the letter because the manager needs it for today's conference.

Look for gobbledygook in every draft. Use the simplest possible language to express your ideas. Readers will appreciate your straightforward style.

⟳ ON YOUR OWN: For practice eliminating gobbledygook from your writing, try the exercises on pages 151–153.

Are your sentences streamlined, active, and free of gobbledygook?

Now that you've edited your sentences, you can look more closely at the words themselves. Proceed to the next issue in the editing process: word choice.

Check Words

CHOOSE THE APPROPRIATE TONE   Tone is how you sound on paper—for example, serious, critical, or warm. Like tone of voice, the tone of your writing should be appropriate to the situation—to your particular reader and subject matter.

Reviewing the answers to the questions on your Focus Sheet will help you to reach out to your readers. The answers will determine the best tone to adopt. Choose your words to fit your reader's personality and background. You probably change the way you talk depending on the person you're with; why not do the same in your writing? Compare the tone of these two report titles:

> "Benefits of Acquiring the XLC Multicopier at Teletrix, Inc."
> "How the Purchase of the XLC Multicopier Would Save Time, Money, and Energy at Teletrix, Inc."

In the first one, the tone is remote and abstract. The tone of the second title is more lively and reflects an awareness that the reader is one of the decision makers on the issue.

When you have a choice, be friendly and informal

Business writing is changing in the direction of informality and straightforwardness. The friendlier and more "real" you sound, the better chance you have of relating to your reader. Be formal only when you feel it's the best way to reach your reader. Modernize your language by avoiding stuffy sentences like, "Should you require further assistance, please do not hesitate to write to my attention."

As Winston Churchill said, "The short words are best." The following list shows some modern alternatives to the worn-out words and phrases that sound so pretentious today:

INSTEAD OF:	USE:	INSTEAD OF:	USE:
		we would like to ask that	please
nevertheless	but	for the reason that	because
terminate	end	are of the opinion	believe
utilize	use	for the purpose of	for, to
deem	think	prior to	before
assistance	help	despite the fact that	although, though
converse	talk	in view of the fact that	because, since
forward	send, mail	in order to	to
advise	tell	subsequent to	after
indicate	show	with reference to	about
reside	live	on the occasion of	when
		during the course of	during
		along the lines of	like
		succeed in making	make
		make use of	use
		have need for	need
		give consideration to	consider
		initiate, or commence	begin, start

Tautologies

When you use a tautology, you're repeating yourself unnecessarily. Watch out for the following redundancies:

advanced ahead	important essentials	surrounding circumstances
attached hereto	just exactly	
at this point in time	merge together	reduce down
basic fundamentals	mutual cooperation	resume again
brief in duration	necessary requisite	round in shape
both together	plan in advance	seems apparent
cooperate together	protrude out	still continue
enclosed herein	in the same way as described	true facts
final ending		ultimate end
hopeful optimism	one A.M. in the morning	young juveniles

◑ ON YOUR OWN: To test your skill in choosing the appropriate tone, try the exercises in "Quiz Yourself" on page 153.

Detecting excessive formality in letters

There are many things wrong with this letter, but the big problem is that it's too formal. Circle all the words or phrases that should be changed or eliminated to improve the tone.

January 23, 1999

Richard McKinney
Manufacturer's Representative
Fogg Smoke Warning Systems
773 South Rodeo Drive
Los Angeles, CA 90000

Dear Mr. McKinney:

I wish to thank you for your prompt reply to my urgent telephone message of last week depicting the grave situation at hand. As you are no doubt aware, it is an absolute necessity for the safety of our patients and our entire staff to have an extensive and dependable smoke warning system. Because of the inavailability of your customary repairman, Mr. Al S. Besto, we are compelled to hire a nonwarranteed service firm. To be sure, an ounce of prevention is worth a pound of cure.

As you requested, I am forwarding a list of the rooms where the breakdowns occur most frequently. I am also enclosing a copy of the hospital floor plan, upon which I have noted the areas experiencing different types of breakdowns. Note: In some rooms (circled in red) the alarms ring at twenty-minute intervals, certainly not conducive to the healing atmosphere of a hospital.

Also, another problem has arisen since we last corresponded. On several smoke detectors, the flashing light that is supposed to accompany the alarm lights up independently from said alarm. This has had particularly distressing consequences in Ward E, where countless patients have complained about flashing lights disturbing them late at night. It is expected that you will find this situation as intolerable as we do. At this point in time, no other flaws appear to exist.

Lastly, with respect to the warranty. Clearly, we cannot wait for Mr. Besto to repair the smoke warning system, since he is hopelessly busy. Although I am cognizant that the Fogg policy normally covers expenses only when the repair work is done by our dealer—i.e., Mr. Besto—I presume that the policy will be relaxed in this disturbing circumstance, allowing us to engage an alternative firm. Would you be so kind as to make confirmation of this in writing?

I trust that you will contact me pursuant to these pressing issues at your earliest convenience. Your assistance is greatly appreciated.

Very truly yours,

Hiram Frost
Vice President
Physical Plant Safety

How did you do?

Compare your responses with those below. Did you pick out most of the problem areas?

January 23, 1999

Richard McKinney
Manufacturer's Representative
Fogg Smoke Warning Systems
773 South Rodeo Drive
Los Angeles, CA 90000

Dear Mr. McKinney:

I wish to thank you for your prompt reply to my urgent telephone message of last week depicting the grave situation at hand. As you are no doubt aware, it is an absolute necessity for the safety of our patients and our entire staff to have an extensive and dependable smoke warning system. Because of the inavailability of your customary repairman, Mr. Al S. Besto, we are compelled to hire a nonwarranteed service firm. To be sure, an ounce of prevention is worth a pound of cure.

As you requested, I am forwarding a list of the rooms where the breakdowns occur most frequently. I am also enclosing a copy of the hospital floor plan upon which I have noted the areas experiencing different types of breakdowns. Note: In some rooms (circled in red) the alarms ring at twenty-minute intervals, certainly not conducive to the healing atmosphere of a hospital.

Also, another problem has arisen since we last corresponded. On several smoke detectors, the flashing light that is supposed to accompany the alarm lights up independently from said alarm. This has had particularly distressing consequences in Ward E, where countless patients have complained about flashing lights disturbing them late at night. It is expected that you will find this situation as intolerable as we do. At this point in time, no other flaws appear to exist.

Lastly, with respect to the warranty. Clearly, we cannot wait for Mr. Besto to repair the smoke warning system, since he is hopelessly busy. Although I am cognizant that the Fogg policy normally covers expenses only when the repair work is done by our dealer—i.e., Mr. Besto—I presume that the policy will be relaxed in this disturbing circumstance, allowing us to engage an alternative firm. Would you be so kind as to make confirmation of this in writing?

I trust that you will contact me pursuant to these pressing issues at your earliest convenience. Your assistance is greatly appreciated.

Very truly yours,

Hiram Frost
Vice President
Physical Plant Safety

Now try rewriting the letter yourself in a friendly and informal tone. Change or remove pompous, old-fogy phrases while retaining as much of the meaning as possible. Our first draft follows. How does it compare with yours?

FIRST DRAFT

January 23, 1999

Richard McKinney
Manufacturer's Representative
Fogg Warning Systems
773 South Rodeo Drive
Los Angeles, CA 90000

RE: Approval needed for repair of smoke alarms

Dear Mr. McKinney:

Thank you for your prompt reply to my phone call describing our problems with our Fogg smoke alarms. As you are aware, it is necessary for the safety of our patients and our entire staff to have an extensive and dependable smoke warning system. Because your customary repair man, Mr. Al S. Besto, is unavailable, we must hire a nonwarranteed service firm to maintain the system.

As you asked, I am sending a list of the rooms where the breakdowns occur most frequently. I am also enclosing a copy of the hospital floor plan on which I have noted the areas that have had different types of breakdowns. You'll notice that in some rooms (circled in red) the alarms ring at twenty-minute intervals, obviously disturbing the quiet that patients need.

Also, another problem has come up since last week. On several smoke detectors, the flashing light that is supposed to come on with the alarm lights up independently from it. This has been particularly upsetting in Ward E, where many patients have complained about the flashing lights disturbing them late at night. We are sure that you find this situation as intolerable as we do.

Last, about the warranty: Clearly, we cannot wait for Mr. Besto to repair the smoke warning system, since he is extremely busy. Although I know that the Fogg policy normally covers expenses only when the repair work is done by our dealer, Mr. Besto, I expect that the policy will be relaxed in this case, allowing us to hire another company. Will you please confirm this in writing?

Please call me about these pressing issues before Wednesday at 4:30 P.M. We appreciate your help.

Very truly yours,

Hiram Frost
Vice President
Physical Plant Safety

Edit for Clarity, Conciseness, and Accuracy

Rewriting the Fogg Letter

It's important to write so that your reader understands exactly what you mean and knows exactly what action you expect. Use words that are precise and that imply action. In the Fogg letter, this straightforward approach worked as follows:

1. The header "RE:" appears below the inside address to help introduce the reader to the situation.
2. In the first paragraph we substituted plainer language to state the problem clearly.
3. In paragraphs two, three, and four, we eliminated redundancies ("absolute"), pompous words ("said"), and overstatement ("countless"). We streamlined by weeding out useless words ("At this point in time") and theatrical words ("hopelessly," "in this disturbing circumstance").
4. In paragraph four, we clarified the action requested and changed the note of thanks from passive to active voice for greater impact.

Is there still room for improvement?

Yes. I think you'll agree that the version of the Fogg letter on page 89 is better than my first draft. Why? Because this version does more than just eliminate words or substitute one word or phrase for another. It uses a more natural, direct style, sounding like what you would *say* to Richard McKinney if you were delivering the message in person. Also, we've added headlines and moved the bottom line to the top.

Adopt a modern tone

Fifty years ago, a formal tone was proper for business letters and memos. Today, the polite formality of the past is often taken for coldness or snobbishness. If, for example, you are writing to ask for someone's help, you don't want to sound distant. It is better to use the lighter and friendlier words of your daily speech.

On page 90 are two memos written by an office supervisor asking for help from her employees in solving a problem. Which one do you think will receive a better response?

January 23, 1999

Richard McKinney
Manufacturer's Representative
Fogg Warning Systems
773 South Rodeo Drive
Los Angeles, CA 90000

RE: Please approve repairs to smoke alarms

Dear Mr. McKinney:

Thank you for replying quickly to my phone call describing the problems with our Fogg smoke alarms.

Exception to warranty needed

Since your customary repair man, Mr. Al S. Besto, is unavailable, we must hire a nonwarranteed service firm to repair our system. We cannot wait for Mr. Besto to repair the smoke warning system. Although the Fogg policy normally covers expenses only when the repair work is done by our dealer, I expect that Fogg will relax the policy in this case, so that we can hire another company.

Location of breakdowns

As you asked, I am sending a list of the rooms where the breakdowns occur most often. I am also enclosing a copy of the hospital floor plan and have noted the areas that have had different types of breakdowns. You'll see that in some rooms (circled in red) the alarms ring at twenty-minute intervals, obviously disturbing our patients.

New problem

Another problem has come up since last week. On several smoke detectors, the flashing light, which is supposed to come on when the alarm sounds, lights up on its own. This has upset patients, especially in Ward E, where many have complained that the flashing lights disturb them late at night. We are sure that you find this situation as intolerable as we do.

Actions requested

- Please call me to discuss these problems before Wednesday at 4:30 P.M.
- If you can okay the exception to your policy, please initial this letter and return it to me to confirm our agreement.

Thank you for helping to ensure the safety of the patients and staff of our hospital.

Sincerely,

Hiram Frost
Vice President
Physical Plant Safety

> **BEFORE**
>
> DATE: May 12, 1999
> TO: Unicomp Staff
> FROM: Bea Bland
> RE: Noise level in the break rooms
>
> There has been great concern expressed about the growing tension between those personnel who use the break rooms as quiet places to work and those who go to the break rooms to converse. This conflict is counterproductive. The most pressing issue at hand is ascertaining the necessity of establishing quiet break rooms.
>
> This developing tension between those who desire quiet and those who desire freedom to talk has great potential for unsettling the office and reducing worker productivity. It must be addressed without further delay. Suggestions deemed suitable should be submitted to the Human Resources Manager. This matter is of concern to all.

> **AFTER**
>
> DATE: May 12, 1999
> TO: Unicomp Staff
> FROM: Beatrice Bland
> RE: Your suggestions about the break rooms
>
> <u>How can we satisfy everyone?</u>
> Many of you have told me about the growing tension you feel around using the break rooms. Some of you go there to rest and socialize; others use the rooms to rest quietly.
>
> <u>Everyone's ideas are welcome</u>
> What do you think we can do to satisfy everyone? Should we designate one room as a lounge and the other as a quiet room?
>
> We're sure you have other ideas. Since your feelings are important, please take a minute or two to send us your suggestions. If we work together, I'm sure we'll solve this.
>
> Thanks for your cooperation.

Six Steps to Reader-Centered Writing

I'm sure you agree that the second memo is far more likely to result in an amicable solution to the problem than the first. The second uses warmth and understanding to mobilize group spirit. The well-chosen tone shows that the writer understands how to motivate people. In the final sentences, she sets positive expectations, thus increasing the likelihood that her staff will cooperate.

Which letter is more influential?

The letters on pages 92 and 93 were written by two account executives from different advertising companies. Each was trying to convince the Blippo Computer company to contract with her company for an ad campaign. Read each one through and decide which tone you feel is more persuasive. Then fill out the response sheet below:

Marketing Letters Response Sheet

1. Which letter do you think was more influential?

2. List four words describing the first letter.

3. List four words describing the second letter.

4. On whom does the writer focus in the opening of letter 1?

5. On whom does the writer focus in the opening of letter 2?

6. Which approach is more likely to involve and engage the reader?

7. Which closing is more likely to result in a meeting? Why?

Compare our answers on page 157 to yours. Pay special attention to the answer to question 7. Try to adopt similar closing methods for you letters. They work!

TAKE THE POSITIVE APPROACH   Sometimes your tone carries a hidden message to the reader. Are you aware that between the lines you communicate your self-confidence or self-doubt to the reader? Ideas expressed positively are most likely to be positively received by the reader. To get the results you desire, you must convey an attitude of confident expectation.

```
                    VAN SNELL ADVERTISING AGENCY
                         4321 Maple Boulevard
                       Boston, Massachusetts 02215

                                                    January 31, 1999

        Mr. Sanford Blanchard
        Product Development
        Blippo Computer
        1234 Via Mallorca
        San Diego, CA 94654

        Dear Mr. Blanchard:

            Having had a great deal of experience working on advertisements suitable
        for the computer industry, my company, Van Snell Advertising Agency, desires
        to inform you as to the optimum methods for the planning and execution of a
        successful advertising campaign.

            In the past we have been able to assist other computer companies lacking
        the expertise or the facilities to create an advertising campaign to successfully
        reach their intended market. Most companies are of course aware of the suc-
        cessful campaigns we have developed in the past and of the prestige associated
        with the Van Snell Advertising Agency, but a brochure describing our team
        approach to advertising design will be found enclosed.

            It is expected that this proposal will be of interest to you, and that we can
        arrange an interview with you soon.

            We look forward to meeting you.

                                                    Very truly yours,


                                                    Ruth Van Snell
                                                    Account Executive

        RVS:AFM
```

Avoid *no* and *not*

Some people are always cheerful, self-assured, and optimistic. They express themselves positively, both orally and in writing. The rest of us tend to express ourselves
more negatively. And most of the time we don't even notice how negative we
sound. But if you tend to write "Do not waste energy" instead of "Conserve
energy," then you are taking a negative approach.

"Don't take a negative approach!" is my message to you, but it would be better

GOODMAN ADVERTISING AGENCY
10 Hartley Avenue
Boston, Massachusetts 02117

February 2, 1999

Mr. Sanford Blanchard
Product Development
Blippo Computer
1234 Via Mallorca
San Diego, CA 94654

RE: A plan to help you make the XL90 famous

Dear Mr. Blanchard:

Your new personal computer, the XL90, is an important addition to the family of fine quality Blippo computers already improving the lives of its users. But without a well-planned and carefully executed advertising campaign, the XL90 may fail to reach its entire potential market.

My company, Goodman Advertising Agency, is one of the oldest and most successful agencies in the country. Our experienced and talented team of marketing research analysts, graphic artists, and writers are skilled in developing the finest campaign for each product they handle.

I would appreciate the opportunity to meet with you and discuss how our team may be of unique service to you. May I suggest June 5 at 2:00 P.M.? I'll call soon to to see if you have time for a short meeting.

Cordially,

Alice Goodman
Account Executive

AG:afm

to say, "Accentuate the positive." It is always more persuasive to suggest what you want than what you don't want. For example, which closing do you prefer?

"Perhaps you won't object to my suggestions. Maybe you'll try to spot negative words and replace them with something less negative."

or:

"I'm sure you'll agree with my suggestions and replace negative words with positive ones."

Edit for Clarity, Conciseness, and Accuracy

ON YOUR OWN: Look over some of your recent letters and memos to see if you suffer from "the negative approach." If you find an abundance of *no*s and *not*s, they could be a signal. Watch for this weakness in future writing.

BE SPECIFIC   One day Tom LeBlanc was working on a memo describing market response to his company's recently developed personal computer, the SLXQ. He had discussed the trends, growth indicators, and general market response. Using sentences like these, he tried to explain why the sales were not as high as predicted:

> The SLXQ has not met with the high degree of public acceptance predicted. Many customers seem to find the equipment too intimidating or cumbersome to learn to operate.

While this is useful information, it is very general and abstract. It needs to be followed with actual examples in order to come alive. To maintain reader interest and to clarify his point, Tom should follow this statement with a real-life example— perhaps the story of Mr. Z, in Houston, who bought an SLXQ only to discover that it was too difficult to operate.

Anecdotes and examples illustrate your abstract ideas, making them come alive. Without examples, your writing will seem dry or overly intellectual. Another problem with excessively abstract writing is that it can be easily misinterpreted. Consider this sentence:

> The atmosphere in the conference room contributed to the outcome of the meeting.

Does it mean:

> The hostility and backbiting among the committee members in the conference room contributed to the rejection of the proposal.

Or does it mean:

> The supportive atmosphere in the conference room contributed to the exceptionally productive meeting.

Whenever possible, choose concrete words to express your ideas. Abstract writing is open to many interpretations, all potentially inaccurate. Therefore, make a real effort to clarify your ideas so that the reader understands your intention. Give examples and add words that create a picture in the reader's mind. Words that relate to the senses—sight, sound, touch, and smell—evoke the strongest response.

Here are a few examples of abstract sentences followed by more concrete versions. Notice how much more helpful the second sentence is.

Abstract:	The unit is malfunctioning.
Concrete:	The freezer isn't making ice cubes.
Abstract:	He amassed major input to determine the functional requirements for console construction.
Concrete:	He interviewed many experts to learn how to build the console.
Abstract:	If a situation like this occurs in the future, please involve others in the office before taking action.
Concrete:	If you ever find the office door unlocked again, please ask people about it before calling in the FBI.
Abstract:	Due to extenuating circumstances, we will have to delay introduction of our new product line for a while.
Concrete:	We've decided to delay introduction of our new product line for six months while we iron out a kink in the propulsion system.

How to lower the abstraction level in technical writing

The technical writers we meet are challenged by having to explain information unfamiliar to their readers. Yet they are the greatest sinners when it comes to being abstract. Some writers in the technical world feel that giving examples and making creative comparisons is unprofessional. It's not. A real professional helps the reader any way he can. When trying to explain an abstraction like aerodynamics, a good writer will use a comparison as simple as the wings of birds.

Abstract Obfuscation Exercise
Directions: The passage that follows is too abstract—it needs some concrete examples. Put an X between any sentences where an example would help:

> When writing a résumé, you may find it hard to decide how much information to offer about your education. The more professional experience you have, the less you need to say about your training. Technical language should be kept to a minimum, since it can be inadvertently intimidating or confusing. Extracurricular activities and personal interests should not be given excessive attention on a résumé. Details of previous job experience should include a concise yet comprehensive description of responsibilities. Under the heading "Selected Accomplishments," you can list achievements that don't seem to fit in anywhere else.

Take a look at the same passage, this time with examples inserted. Aren't you surprised at how much difference the examples make?

Education: How much to include?

When writing a résumé, you may find it hard to decide how much information to offer about your education. The more professional experience you have, the less you need to say about your training. For example, if you have worked in your profession for many years, you need not list courses taken in your college career. For an electrical engineer who is applying for a higher-paid job, a simple statement of his or her degrees and the names of schools attended suffices.

Beware of getting too technical

Technical language should be kept to a minimum, since it can be inadvertently intimidating or confusing. A young chemist looking for a nonlaboratory job should not merely list courses with titles such as "Ionization of Crystalline Particles in Saline Solutions," which may give a misleading impression of primary career interests. He should also mention courses in marketing or management if they are relevant.

Should you mention personal activities or interests?

Extracurricular activities and personal interests should not be given excessive attention on a résumé. Interviewers are unlikely to be overly impressed with a detailed account of an applicant's high school debate team's victories, summer hiking itineraries, or musical preferences. A brief mention of major interests at the end of a résumé, under a heading such as "Activities and Interests" may provide an employer with some helpful impressions of the individual and offer an opening for informal discussion during an interview.

Summarizing your job experience

Details of previous job experience should include a concise yet comprehensive description of responsibilities. Clearly indicate dates of employment, titles, significant duties, number of staff supervised, scope of budget, special reports, projects completed, and any promotions.

Include miscellaneous achievements separately

Under the heading "Selected Accomplishments" you can list achievements that don't seem to fit in anywhere else. For example, you might mention awards, volunteer work, or special learning experiences. This category is especially helpful because it frees you from giving the traditional year-by-year account of your past.

Notice how the addition of examples enhanced your understanding of the original article. Suddenly, the piece came to life. Be watchful for places in your own writing where an example would reach out to your readers and add to their understanding.

HOW TO REDUCE SEXIST LANGUAGE   Traditionally, the pronoun *his* has been used to refer to men and women alike. Consider a sentence like this: "Every employee should turn in his work." Let's be realistic: using this sentence will raise eyebrows today. You may be considered insensitive, or even run the risk that women will ignore the request. For many objectors, resorting to traditional grammar rules to defend the use of *his* won't get you off the hook.

S/he doesn't solve the problem

To meet the need to refer to women directly, writers created *s/he* and *his/hers* or awkwardly referred to both *him and her.* But resorting to these cumbersome usages to avoid offending women can also offend.

Avoid the problem: where possible, use plural pronouns instead of singular ones

Notice how plural pronouns let you use the neutral *their,* while singular pronouns force you to choose between *his* and *her.*

Plural subjects	. . . require . . .	plural pronouns.
Employees	should turn in	their work.
People	should turn in	their work.
All architects	should turn in	their work.

Singular subjects	. . . require . . .	singular pronouns.
Each employee	should turn in	his or her work.
Everyone	should turn in	his or her work.
Anybody	should turn in	his or her work.
Anyone	should turn in	his or her work.

Chairman and salesman are risky, too

Women frequently chair committees, work in sales and perform myriad other roles once reserved for men. Even though the suffix *-man* traditionally includes women in these roles, writers have invented words like *chairperson* and *salesperson.* We recommend substituting *person* for *man* for two reasons. First, you avoid having to choose between using *salesman* or *saleswoman.* But more important, you're more likely to be accurate: sometimes you really don't know who the chairperson will be.

Are you satisfied with your word choice and tone?

Are you sure that they:
- are right for your audience?
- reflect a positive approach?

Yes? Then, take another step in the right direction and be sure you're writing at the right level for your reader.

Measure the Readability of Your Writing

When you measure readability, you're determining how easy or difficult it is to understand your writing. By controlling the reading level, you minimize the risk of being misunderstood.

At what level should I write?

That's like asking how fast you should drive. The answer, of course, depends on the situation. However, the "when-in-doubt-slow-down" principle applies to writers and drivers alike. When in doubt, make your writing easier to read, not harder.

We recommend ninth level writing for business documents. This standard suggests that you avoid long words and keep sentence length at about 15 words. Focusing on the length of your words and sentences will help you adjust your writing level. If you suspect that your reader may lack time, interest, or enthusiasm, make your writing as easy to read as possible.

Learn to adjust readability based on your reader and purpose

In business, it's valuable to know how to adjust for readability. You may find yourself writing everything from a summary report for a manager, to a feasibility study for engineers, to a set of procedures for clerical trainees. If you have a number of readers or you don't know who your readers are, stay below the ninth level.

This book is written at the ninth level, and many of the sample letters we've used are at the seventh level. Even *The Macintosh Advisor,* a technical book written for experienced users of the Macintosh computer, reads at the eighth level. Most people are surprised to learn that writers of technical information can keep readability levels low.

Reading levels of familiar publications

The following list scores the readability level of familiar periodicals and documents:

MAGAZINES AND NEWSPAPERS

The Atlantic	12 (difficult)
The Wall Street Journal	11
The New York Times	10
Los Angeles Times	10
Business Week	10
Time magazine	10
Reader's Digest	8
Boston Globe	8
U.S.A. Today	7
People magazine	6 (easy)

SPEECHES

Winston Churchill's	6
Lincoln's Gettysburg Address	10

SOFTWARE DOCUMENTATION

WordPerfect	9
DBase III+	9.5

How do I measure readability?

To see how to derive a readability score on your own writing, refer to Fry's Readability Graph in Appendix C on page 166.

Software programs make measuring readability easy

A number of excellent programs that include readability analysis are on the market. Rightwriter, MacProof, FullWrite, and Fogfinder compute the readability level for you. They calculate the average sentence length (words per sentence) and the average word length (syllables per word) as the basis for the reading-level calculation. Some programs will even search for editing or grammar errors. A software store or consultant can recommend programs suitable for your needs.

The problem of technical writing

Sometimes when you're writing on a technical subject, you cannot simplify the level of your writing even if you want to. If your readers are familiar with the subject matter, you probably shouldn't worry. But if you're trying to communicate technical information to nontechnical managers, stockholders, or clients, be extremely careful to define or translate terms they may not recognize.

One hint: Pay special attention to shortening your sentences and use comparisons or concrete examples liberally. The authors of *The Macintosh Advisor* used this technique and wrote a level-8 paragraph to explain what an operating system is:

If someone asked you what you're doing now, you'd say, "I'm reading a book." Yet, even though reading is the main "program" you're using, behind the scenes your body is doing lots of other things: breathing air; circulating blood, maybe tapping your foot unconsciously, or scratching your head.

Computers work pretty much the same way. Even while they're running one main application, like a word-processing program or a spreadsheet, behind the scenes a set of programs known as the operating system is taking care of basic housekeeping procedures—chores like starting up and shutting down the computer; or listing, displaying, and copying individual files.*

You're not writing to entertain or to prove your literary talent

Business writing is not literature. Readers of business documents go to the subject line, the purpose statement, and may or may not read more than the first sentence of every paragraph. You want your readers to get the point quickly, so write to inform, not to impress.

Are you satisfied with the readability of your writing?

If so, then there's just one step left before you have a final draft to present to your typist. This last step ensures the clarity and accuracy of the document you send to your readers.

Proofread

Proofread as if your career depended on it. It might. Sending out a letter without proofreading carefully beforehand is like walking into an important meeting dressed to the teeth—except for those muddy running shoes you forgot to change after jogging to the office in the morning. At best, people will think you're not good with details. Is this an image that will advance your career?

Who's responsible?

Passing the buck is often easier than accepting responsibility. The typist will say that the writer ought to proofread; the writer will say it's the typist's job. If your name is on the bottom of a letter, you are ultimately responsible for correcting every misspelling, typo, or grammar/punctuation error—in short, every detail.

Enlist help

If you wish, you may ask your typist or a trusted colleague to use the "Be Your Own Editor" Checklist to check your work for errors. Your typist should at least help in the following ways:
  • mentioning any errors noticed

*Reproduced with permission of the publisher, Howard W. Sams & Company, Indianapolis, *The MacIntosh Advisor* by Cynthia Harriman and Bencion Calica, copyright © 1986.

- checking all questionable spellings (easy if you have a computer program)
- typing or printing first drafts double-spaced for easy editing.

Every company I visit has different norms about how involved in proofreading the typist should be. Do what feels right in your work environment.

Check your spelling

Everyone needs to use a reliable, up-to-date dictionary. Even good spellers need to look up words occasionally. Making a spelling error isn't an awful mistake—but not catching one can be.

Use the spelling cheat sheet

On page 163, you'll find a list of words most often misspelled by business writers. Use the list to help you identify problem words and to check correct spelling; consult a dictionary whenever you are uncertain about any word.

Read your draft slowly and carefully to spot errors

You must read at a pace that allows you to understand every word. If you read too quickly, you'll miss spelling errors like this simple omission of the letter *a* in the following sentence:

He wrote the specifictions for the project.

Use the spellchecker to back you up

Those of us with word processors can use the spellcheck function to correct our spelling. Beware: spellcheck will won't catch mistakes like the ones in these sentences:

Their were tears strolling down there faces.
He works for that import/expert bank.
All the principles of the law firm were formerly indicted.

Look for errors in grammar and punctuation

You don't need to be an expert in grammar and punctuation to write. You already know more than you might think about correct English because you use it every day. Try reading your draft aloud and you'll hear many hard-to-catch mistakes.

Boost your grammar confidence level

Part Three of this book is largely devoted to instruction and exercises in grammar and punctuation. Use the "Quiz Yourself in Grammar" sections to review the basics. There's extra help, too, in case you have trouble with any particular aspect of grammar or punctuation.

Each piece of writing that leaves your office reflects your intelligence, thoroughness, and effectiveness. You are sending an image of yourself into the world. You'll find that the more polished and neat your correspondence, the more respect you'll gain. Save yourself needless embarrassment: appear as successful as you are!

Use your Step 6 checklist

You've come to the end of the editing process. Remember, the "Be Your Own Editor" Checklist on pages 65–66 makes an excellent desktop reference for editing your documents. Use this checklist to produce a final draft that presents your ideas in the best possible light. The more you use the checklist, the more automatic the editing process will become. Soon editing will be a comfortable habit rather than a tedious chore.

EDIT ON SCREEN WITH A WORD PROCESSOR

Why do some people avoid writing? Usually it's not the creative first phase they dislike—it's the tedium of copying and recopying drafts. Editing on screen with a word processor is a simpler, quicker, more productive task than editing the traditional way. You can make changes easily yet always have a clean draft to work on—a neat, legible draft that allows you to see instantly what the changes look like.

Say good-bye to busywork

If you edit on screen, words, lines, or sections will not be crossed out. There won't be any lines and arrows showing what paragraphs you want moved. You won't have to squeeze additions or changes between lines and in margins. Best of all, you will not need to interpret these hieroglyphics for your typist or yourself. Using a word processor, you will find yourself only a few changes away from the final product much more quickly than you ever imagined.

Consult your user's manual

Once you learn the commands and functions of on-screen editing, you will quickly become proficient. By pressing a key or clicking a mouse, you will instantly:
- delete or insert lines
- type over existing lines
- move words, phrases, sentences, paragraphs, or whole sections
- change typeface and style
- indent lines or paragraphs
- search for words you have repeated within your document
- check your spelling

A few "don'ts"
- Don't create new errors while making corrections. For example, carefully plan major deletions and insertions.

- Don't expect your automatic spellchecker to spot *your* as a misspelling when you really meant *you're*.

If you have access to a word processor, by all means start to use it for editing as well as writing your draft. It's a guaranteed way to cut your writing time almost in half. But, whether you use a word processor or edit the traditional way, you will probably agree that being a sharp editor is perhaps the most important part of writing well.

PART TWO

Writing to Influence

*The difficulty is not
to affect your reader, but to
affect him precisely as you wish.*
ROBERT LOUIS STEVENSON

Negotiations and Strategies

More and more often we find ourselves negotiating on paper for the things we want—for example, a budget increase for the department or a preliminary contract with a client. Whenever you are involved in this sort of give-and-take, remember this rule of thumb: always ask for more than you really want.

Bargaining

If you are bargaining for five items, you are likely to end up with the three that really matter to you. If you start out asking for only the three things you truly want, you have nothing left to bargain with. Bargaining means trading off some of your requests in the expectation that the other party will do the same.

No matter how much you like or respect the person or group you are negotiating with, you must also respect yourself enough to win what you need. This will ensure your sense of a fair negotiation. To create an atmosphere of ongoing, friendly give-and-take, begin negotiations with a few requests that you know you can concede if necessary.

Creating a win-win situation

Whenever you're negotiating, whether orally or in writing, try to take a positive approach. By this I mean offering enough concessions so that both parties can feel they won. This goal is particularly important in large corporations where you are constantly negotiating with the same people. The relationship is usually more important than winning every time.

Don't be tempted to use "win-at-any-cost" power tactics if you must face the same person or group a week later on a different issue. How will it feel to work together after the smoke clears? Plan in advance what you can offer to create a situation where each side feels happy with the outcome. As a newly promoted manager, you may have only one chance to learn this lesson. Success is not always to the strongest.

Letters of agreement

You've reached an oral understanding with someone, and now it's time to confirm your agreement in writing. Having negotiated successfully this far, you may feel that the final coup would be to maneuver the other party into writing the letter of agreement. Resist this temptation.

By writing the letter yourself, you retain more power over the situation. The subtleties of the agreement will be construed in your favor, and any issues that remain in doubt will appear from your point of view.

On the other hand, if you leave the agreement writing to the other person, you are much more likely to be in a weak position. You might have to renegotiate points that the writer misunderstood or left out completely, intentionally or not. You'll be much happier with the results of any negotiation if you can reserve the writing of the agreement letter for yourself.

Stalling for time

Sometimes you can use people's dislike of the writing process to gain time for yourself. Here's how one busy vice president named Frank did it:

One day Frank was approached by an enthusiastic but misguided manager with a suggestion for improving the department. The suggestion seemed unworkable, and Frank was hopelessly busy the moment the manager chose to make his proposal.

Frank's reply? "Put it in writing, please. And then we'll talk." This was a good response to the situation because it forced the manager to think out his ideas more clearly and to present them in the best possible light. It gave Frank time to ponder the unlikely idea a bit, avoiding an immediate negative reply that could discourage the manager if it seemed too hasty.

Executives often use their subordinates' dislike of writing to maneuver around dealing with unwanted suggestions. Many a proposal has died a natural death when its originators felt it was just too much trouble to put it in writing. Asking that any oral negotiation be documented will usually slow down the entire process and give you more time to plan your response.

Warnings

One of the less pleasant aspects of being a manager is having to document substandard performance by employees. But in today's business climate, it's often necessary.

The "shotgun" approach

Too often when managers have a gripe about something, they send a "warning" memo to *every* employee, guilty or not. Although meant to improve a situation, this strategy usually has the opposite effect. Good eggs are insulted; bad eggs are unmoved by such subtleties.

If you must use this technique, a strategic opening sentence will help aim your communication more accurately and effectively. For example: "I know that most of you are extremely punctual, and I appreciate it more than you can imagine. However, a few of you . . ."

The "rifle" approach

Dealing with specific individuals, although tricky, is better in the long run. The innocent will appreciate your take-charge management style; the guilty will get the message. But the direct approach need not be negative or confrontational. Here are some strategies for communicating your concerns in a way that:
- encourages the employee to improve or change
- documents your actions

A. THE ORAL WARNING

Early in the process, use an oral warning. Even the best-written warnings can seem like a blow; at this stage, a *helping* hand works better.

Step #1: Either in a casual setting (over coffee) or a formal setting (your office), sit down with the employee and explain your concerns. Give specific information to back up these concerns: examples, dates, sales records, etc. Lay out the improvements you expect, encouraging the employee to contribute ideas. During this conversation, you can work out "next steps" and deadlines.

Step #2: After this conversation, make notes on:
- date, time, and place of meeting
- concerns you shared with employee and specific proof you presented
- employee's response
- specific improvements expected or agreed upon
- next steps and deadlines

Step #3: Put these notes in a file or log. Later, if you're forced into termination litigation, notes of this kind, if complete, are usually legally acceptable evidence.

B. THE WRITTEN WARNING

If an oral warning is either ineffective or inappropriate, put your concerns in writing for the individual. Here are some tips:
- Keep your tone neutral rather than threatening.
- Stick to the facts: describe your concerns, giving specific examples.
- Avoid judgmental adjectives.

- Focus on the undesirable behaviors instead of criticizing the person.
- Repeat or make an offer to help.
- Be clear about improvements expected.
- Give deadlines and other follow-up planned.

C. THE ANGRY MEMO

Although it can feel cathartic to *write* when you're angry, it's never a good idea to *send* out what you've written in the heat of the moment. If you need the release, go ahead and vent your anger on paper—then toss your document in a drawer until you and the situation have cooled.

When you have calmed down, examine your audience and your purpose objectively. Which approach will accomplish your ultimate purpose:
- a heated tone?
- a neutral tone?
- a cold and distant tone?

Edit your communication accordingly and send with confidence.

D. THE ANONYMOUS TIP

Have you ever received a copied memo from a writer in your company whom you don't even know? Or a memo that at first glance seems irrelevant? Don't instantly dismiss memos like this by assuming that they came from some blunderer suffering from copy-mania. It is possible that such a memo could mean:
- Someone new is evaluating you or your colleagues.
- You or your department has done something serious enough to attract the attention of top management.
- Someone is making a power play that could affect you in some way.
- Someone wants your job.
- Someone mistakenly thinks that you have more authority than you do.

ON THE SUBJECT OF CC'S

Now that carbon paper is out of style, perhaps we should redefine "cc:" to mean courtesy copy. Since the advent of the copy machine, many managers have been "courtesy copied" to death with memos of only the most remote relevance to them. Avoid circulating copies of memos unless they really matter to each person receiving them. People will start ignoring you if you send courtesy copies indiscriminately.

David Ewing, author of *Writing for Results,* asked a top executive for the most important step people might take to improve their written communications. The emphatic reply: "Not writing at all!"*

*David Ewing, *Writing for Results* (New York: John Wiley & Sons, 1974), p.17.

WHO'S ON TOP?

Managers often ask, "How should the list of names of those receiving copies appear at the bottom of a letter? Should they be listed alphabetically or by rank?" Here's the best approach:

- If you are sending copies to people of equal status, arrange the names alphabetically.
- If you are writing to people of widely differing ranks—especially if one person is very high up—you should defer to the top person by listing him or her first. Some organizations are so conservative that it's considered impolite to send a copy to the very top brass: they expect their own freshly typed original. Ask those in the know if this is the situation where you work.

How to Get Action from Your Writing

It all seemed so simple. In your mind you knew clearly what you wanted to ask, you sat down at your terminal and wrote a letter. Simple. Except several weeks later you received a letter that seemed to be written in response to someone else. Maybe the problem was yours. Maybe you weren't as clear as you thought.

An anxious consumer wrote the letter on page 113. His new purchase was defective, and he was trying to get it fixed under the provisions of a company warranty. If you were a customer-relations representative of the Euripides Paper Shredder Company, wouldn't you have been confused?

Don's letter has lots of problems. Even though it probably took him only five minutes to dash off, each follow-up letter that he writes to explain the previous one will take twice as long. He may end up making a costly call to Idaho.

Here are several strategies to ensure a positive response from your letters and to save you from Don's dilemma.

- Make sure you state the subject of your letter in your reference headline after "RE:" If you feel it's not offensive, state the request here instead.
- Begin with your real purpose. Rarely are enclosures or attachments your most important point—so don't begin with them.
- Choose a tone appropriate to the situation. Avoid angry or insinuating remarks if you're writing a complaint. These will get you nowhere.
- Express your positive expectations for cooperation. A note of warmth always helps.
- Supply only enough background material to orient the reader to the situation. More than this might obscure your request.

127 Redwood Rd.
Altoona, RI 02816
Tel. (722) 555-9090

September 19, 1999

The Euripides Paper Shredder Company
Consumer Relations
11540 Columbus Roadway
Melrose, ID 30957

Dear Customer Relations Supervisor:

I am enclosing one of the broken parts from my new desktop paper shredder, but the other part that broke (it had a yellow extension with a red handle), was thrown out by my secretary who got sick of staring at it while I was busy looking for your warranty. The red handle was broken right in two, believe me.

I really appreciate your guarantee to replace broken parts. And I hope that you will make an allowance for my secretary's having thrown out the other broken part instead of understanding that we had to save it.

Thank you very much.

Sincerely,

Don Stipp

- Before you close, be sure your reader knows what to do. Request specific action: what, when, how. Use headlines such as Action Requested, Deadlines, and Next Steps.

Now, pretend that you are Don Stipp, and you just purchased the desktop shredder only to find that two parts were broken. How would you notify the Euripides Paper Shredder Company of your misfortune so that you get your desired action—the replacement of the two defective parts? Try writing a better version. Here's a chance to use the Six Steps.

How did you do?

The "after" letter is our approach. How does your letter compare? Let's examine the contents of the letter. Do you think the reader had these secret thoughts?

AFTER

127 Redwood Rd.
Altoona, RI 02816
Tel. (722) 555-9090

September 19, 1999

The Euripides Paper Shredder Company
Consumer Relations Department
11540 Columbus Roadway
Melrose, ID 30957

RE: Defective Paper Shredder

Dear Customer Relations Supervisor:

<u>Please replace parts</u>

Two days ago, I purchased a new desktop paper shredder, #92131X, manufactured by your company. Unfortunately, the shredder had two broken parts. Since your company has such a fine reputation, I am sure that you will replace the two defective parts as soon as possible, as your warranty promises.

<u>Broken part enclosed</u>

Only one of the broken parts is enclosed. The other, a yellow piece with a red handle attached, was accidentally thrown away. Please accept my word that the second part was broken when I unpacked it.

<u>Speedy action desired</u>

If you have any further questions, please telephone me. I would appreciate your speedy action in delivering the two replacement parts to me. Please call if you can't deliver the parts by October 5.

Thank you for your help with this.

Sincerely,

Don Stipp

I'm sure you'll agree that Don would have saved himself time and achieved the results he sought if he had used the Six Steps to Reader-Centered Writing.

LETTER CONTENT	READER RESPONSE
1. One broken part of the new desktop paper shredder is enclosed.	*1. Unclear explanation.*
2. Secretary threw out other part.	*2. Who cares who did it?*
3. I almost lost your warranty.	*3. A blunderer.*
4. I like your guarantee to replace broken parts.	*4. But do you want your new parts?*

Let's look at the likely reader response to the second letter.

LETTER CONTENT	READER RESPONSE
1. I have a broken paper shredder made by your company.	*1. Aha, I see the problem stated.*
2. It came with two broken parts.	*2. Thanks for the exact details.*
3. . . . a yellow piece with a red handle attached . . .	*3. Parts described as accurately as possible.*
4. Your warranty promises to replace them.	*4. Clear expectations.*
5. Any problem, give me a call.	*5. Responsiveness/note of warmth.*
6. Please deliver two replacement parts.	*6. I see what you want.*

Minutes of Meetings

As the official record of meetings, minutes have two primary purposes:
- to document decisions
- to document work assignments

Once approved, they can even serve as evidence in a court of law. Therefore, minutes must be accurate, complete, and clear.

Good minutes get action

Many a meeting has ended with participants feeling much was accomplished, only to find later that no one took action on the decisions. These suggestions are designed to help you write minutes that get results.

Compare these two sets of minutes

Sample 1

These are the minutes of the meeting held in the Pearson Conference Room on January 9, 1991. Joan, Alan, Steve, and Ann met to discuss how Christmas sales went and to talk about how to be better prepared next year. We decided that we just didn't have enough information to discuss things fairly, so we will discuss the topic again in February.

Date:	January 9, 1991
Purpose of Meeting:	To Evaluate Christmas Sales
Attendees:	Joan C. Crimmons Sales Manager Alan Lakes Buyer Steven Jengian Assistant Buyer Ann Gold Assistant Buyer
Topic:	Overall Sales vs. Objectives
Discussion:	1. Steve distributed the attached summary of sales. 2. Ann feels we need more data from our competitors to see if we really did poorly or if our objectives were just too high, given this year's spending.
Next Steps:	• **Alan** will get figures from other retail stores in our area to Joan **by January 29**. • **Joan** will put the topic on the February agenda.

Why is the second set better?

The "after" minutes clearly reflect the decisions made and the persons responsible for taking action. It's much more likely that Alan will get the figures to Joan by the deadline if he receives the second set of minutes.

The author of the second set of minutes used the following guidelines:

1. USE HEADLINES AND A CONSISTENT FORMAT

People refer to minutes to remind them of the outcome of discussions and to remind them about assignments they accepted. Headlines help tremendously. If the meeting is held routinely, establish a consistent set of headlines people will see each time. In addition to the ones used in these sample minutes, consider some of these possibilities:

Motions raised	Arguments against	Actions to be taken
Items postponed	Alternatives discussed	Deadlines
Recommendations	Final decision	Person responsibile
Arguments in favor	Actions taken	

One Board of Directors that met yearly for three days used only the headlines Topic, Discussion, and Action. They installed the format as a "macro" on a portable computer, and each board member took turns recording the minutes. No one felt overworked, and the minutes had a consistent tone, despite the multi-author approach.

2. INCLUDE ONLY A SUMMARY OF THE DISCUSSION

A word-for-word account gets tiresome: just summarize the major points. Give people credit for their ideas, but make sure you don't editorialize or misreport. Avoid judgmental adjectives like *irritated, abrupt,* or *curt.*

3. USE A PROFESSIONAL YET PERSONABLE TONE

You have to be sensitive to the style and culture of your own organization or the group of people meeting. Sometimes humor is called for, sometimes it's not. One creative minute-taker added a <u>Weather</u> headline so he could note, "Rain, finally." He worked for an agriculture supply house.

4. PROVIDE ONLY NECESSARY AND RELEVANT DETAILS, BUT DO BE SPECIFIC

The room you met in probably isn't relevant. However, if a major decision is being considered, it may be helpful to include as many points from the discussion as possible. Vagueness wastes space and will make your minutes less valuable.

5. PROVIDE COMPLETE NAMES AND TITLES

These details take very little extra space and add to the professional tone you want.

6. HIGHLIGHT ACTION ITEMS AND DEADLINES

These are vital to the document. Clearly presented action items guarantee that attendees understand their commitments. Well-written minutes assure them that their meeting time was well spent.

Remember, headlines offer easy access

If you need to refer to minutes six months from now, you won't have to read every word to find the information you need. The headlines will save everyone a lot of time.

Team Writing: Two Case Histories

What is team writing?

Major assignments such as project or audit reports, proposals, or position papers usually go to groups of people rather than to individuals. Even if an individual has primary responsibility for a document, several layers of review usually precede approval and sign-off. You are "team writing" any time more than one person must be involved before the document is final.

Some people find it difficult to write with others. Some welcome the opportunity, especially experienced writers, who recognize the value of others' input. Team writing presents an opportunity to capitalize on all the brains and talent available. By developing your skills, you will find both the process and the final product more satisfying.

What role do you play on the team?

From project to project, your assignment may differ. Even within one project, you might sometimes write, sometimes edit. Who needs team writing skills?

- the manager who assigned the work (delegator)
- groups preparing a document for senior management (writers)
- peer reviewers
- a single "ghostwriter" creating material for another's signature

Overview: clarify, communicate, coordinate, and critique supportively

CLARIFY ROLES

As basic as it sounds, sometimes teams don't have a clear understanding of who will be drafting, who will be editing, and who will be signing off on what sections. Clarify roles, responsibilities, and deadlines as soon as possible.

COMMUNICATE

Writers and delegators need to communicate their expectations and feelings to each other. If you are having trouble with either your team members or your assignment, talk it out with those involved. Keeping your concerns a secret is almost always counterproductive.

COORDINATE

For efficiency, writers and reviewers need to coordinate their work.

Delegators: Consult the writers before setting deadlines.

Writers: Avoid making promises you can't keep. If you think a deadline is unrealistic, try to negotiate a new one.

Reviewers: Be specific about the time you need to review carefully. Keep writers and delegators informed about your progress.

CRITIQUE SUPPORTIVELY

It's important to comment honestly on each other's work. It's equally important to do so in a way that acknowledges people's feelings and their contributions. Later, we'll offer specific tips on critiquing supportively.

Use the Six Steps as your common language

Keeping the preceding overview of the team writing process in mind, let's look at how the Six Steps will propel you through the group-writing effort. Experience proves that if the team completes the planning phases together, the writing and editing go more smoothly.

Step 1: Completing the Focus Sheet

What is the most common complaint we hear from team writers? People waste countless hours on misdirected work because initial goals were not adequately explained. To prevent this, have your whole team (or at minimum the key players) fill out the Focus Sheet that follows. This is an essential step at your first meeting for teams of any size.

The key questions on the Focus Sheet are, *"Why are we writing this?"* and *"Who will be reading it?"* Answer all questions completely before you move forward. The more time you invest in Step 1—defining your purpose and analyzing your audience—the more time you'll save later.

What if you can't schedule a meeting?

Delegator: Once you've assigned a writing task, the Focus Sheet can help you minimize afterthoughts. By answering the key questions, you will help the writer or team start with a clear understanding of the project.

For Team Writing or Ghostwriting
use this

Focus Sheet

1. **Purpose:**
   - Why are we writing this? _____
   - What do we want the reader to do? _____

2. **Audience:**
   - Who is/are our reader(s)? _____
   _____
   - What is the reader's role? _____
   _____
   - What does the reader know about the subject? _____
   _____
   - How will the reader react? _____
   _____
   - What is our reader's style? Should we adjust to it? _____
   _____
   - How will the reader use this document? _____
   _____
   - Whom should we include in this mailing? _____

3. **Bottom line:**

   If the reader were to forget everything else, what one key point do we want remembered?

   _____
   _____
   _____

4. **Strategy:**
   - Should *we* be writing this? At *this* time?
     Would a phone call or meeting be more effective?
   - Should *we* send this at all? Are *we* too late?
   - Is someone else communicating the same information?
     Should we check with that person?
   - Is our method of transmission the best? For example, should we be using electronic mail, traditional mail, or fax?

© 1986 Deborah Dumaine

Team Writing: Two Case Studies

121

Ghostwriter: Before you tackle the project, use the Focus Sheet to interview the delegator (or the one whose sign-off you need). Also, ask any questions you have about roles, deadlines, or expectations.

Writers: If all of your schedules don't coincide, schedule a meeting for those who can get together. Each absentee can fill out the Focus Sheet individually and send it to the meeting.

Step 2: Generating Ideas as a Team

Delegator: Your participation is especially important in this phase: you may discover some ideas that haven't come out yet. The more you can be involved up front, the better.

Writers: Involve as many team members as possible in generating ideas. Use one or more of the Start-up Strategies. If the whole group can't get together, have each person work alone on a strategy. Then the team can compare notes and integrate ideas.

Steps 3 & 4: Grouping and Sequencing Information

At this phase, you create the outline to guide your writing of the document. Until people are happy with the skeleton, you are not ready to flesh it out. To complete Steps 3 and 4 efficiently, limit the number of people who work on them to one or two. They can propose to the team appropriate categories and headlines for the ideas generated during Step 2. Then the team can work together to finalize headlines and sequence.

Review your ideas or outline with the delegator

Writers: Before you write the draft, check in with the delegator. If a meeting is not feasible, have a phone conversation to discuss key decisions or ask for written comments in the margins of the outline.

EFFICIENCY TIP: USE THE IDEA DRAFT

Both our audit and our business-development clients work on tight deadlines. To avoid wasting time perfecting a first draft without the manager's input, they use the Idea Draft. Emphasizing content and sequence only, the Idea Draft is a list of ideas or a traditional outline, generated from a Start-up Strategy.

Typically, writers submit first drafts to be sure they're on the right track. If they learn they've made many errors, they're usually frustrated at all the time and effort they've wasted. The Idea Draft offers an advance check-in to prevent frustration.

How to use the Idea Draft

When you use the Idea Draft, both parties make a deal. Here's how it works:

Delegator: Promises to comment only on the *content* and *sequence* of the Idea Draft. Won't criticize grammar or writing style. This form of supportive critiquing frees the writers to keep their part of the deal.

Writers: Agree to all the relevant points in a logical sequence. Won't devote the usual time to editing and grammar.

When to use the time-saving Idea Draft

- You need to speed up the process on routine writing assignments.
- A writing project is very complex.
- You're just learning the job.

Step 5: Drafting as a Team

Ghostwriter: If you're the lone ghostwriter, go to it. This part of the process is yours.

Writers: Break the project down into sections and assign sections to individuals. Another option is to choose someone to write a draft for group review.

Delegator: If the team is stuck on who-does-what, make assignments yourself.

Step 6: Editing the Draft

Writer: Before giving your work to your fellow writers or the reviewer, do your own Step 6 edit of the document using the "Be Your Own Editor" Checklist. Sharing the draft with a peer may also produce some helpful comments.

              Get distance so that you can look at the draft again with a more objective eye. Try reading it aloud or into a tape recorder. For critical documents, ask someone to read it aloud to you—someone who won't automatically insert the appropriate inflections.

              While you reread your draft or listen to how it sounds, think about how your team members or reviewers will react to the writing. What will they like or dislike? Do their possible reactions suggest changes you could make?

Other team members: Use the "Be Your Own Editor" guidelines on pages 65–66 to edit the team's document carefully before sending it "upstairs" to your delegator/reviewer.

Delegator: Style differences pose problems. You're more likely to get what you want if you give your writers a sample of the approximate tone and style you're after. Our maxim, "Ego is out, strategy is in," can help you achieve a uniform style throughout. In other words, guide the team toward choosing what the audience needs and away from debates about whose style is best.

How to critique supportively

If you have several people who ghostwrite for you, you probably prefer the one whose writing gets your signature on first reading. That's the independent writer! Your job as a delegator is to move all of your writers to that level of independence by critiquing them supportively. However, many editors unwittingly create dependence by correcting their writers' errors rather than teaching them to identify and repair their own.

Viewing your job as one of trainer rather than editor will help you to encourage independence. Train writers to be their own editors by *commenting* on errors rather than fixing them. If you do all the editing, writers will be less inclined to present a complete document to you. Why should they, when they assume you will change it anyway?

Some typical comments

Instead of revising a sentence, write in the margin, "Is your most important point in the best place? Please resequence," or "Please shorten this sentence." If you write "dangling modifier" or "passive voice" in the margin, then the writer can refer to Part Three of this book for an explanation of the errors.

Questions are especially helpful because they get writers to think for themselves:
- "Have you used enough headlines?"
- "Will the reader get the wrong impression here?"
- "What was your intended tone? You sound irritated."

More tips for reviewers

1. Expect writers to critique themselves first. This places the initial burden of editing on them. But more important, it gives them a chance to acknowledge their own possible concerns about the document. This strategy can reduce defensiveness.

For example, if the writer has a chance to say, "I think it takes me too long to get to the point," the editor can then say, "Well, let's work together on that one." This sets a much more supportive tone for the conversation and makes a writer feel "helped" rather than criticized by the editor's written comments.

2. Watch your timing. Use good judgment in returning your comments, no matter how nondefensive the writer seems to be. No one likes even a supportive critique after receiving some bad news from another side of life.

3. Show model reports to illustrate format as well as style. Examples speak much more clearly than a generalized explanation. Be as specific as you can to help writers understand their goals.

4. Say *something* positive. Even a beginner's work will have something to recommend it. "It's brief and to the point," "Your opener is just what Johnson will want to hear," or "You've got a good start" will set a positive tone for the most problem-filled discussions.

When you're writing comments, try to offer at least one positive tidbit for each page you read. People are less defensive when they know you've appreciated their strengths, even if your job is to help them find their weaknesses. Let writers know where they stand with comments like this: "Your proposal is a strong B—let's turn it into an A."

Give as much positive feedback as you can. We hear writers complain that even when their work is perfect, they get nothing but a signature. It can be demoralizing to spend time perfecting a document, never to bask in the glory of your success.

5. Comment on the writing, not the writer. People naturally feel vulnerable when they submit their writing to someone else. Try to make it clear with your tone that your comments are not personal attacks; you are focusing on what you see on the page.

Your comments on a written document should be subject to the same standards for tone that we recommend in our discussion of editing in Step 6. Be positive, direct, and personable. Sarcasm ("What could you possibly have had in mind here?") crosses the line into criticizing the writer, rather than his or her word choice. "These words don't express your point clearly" is much better.

6. Pay attention to the emotional component. Even when the Six-Step process seems to be going smoothly, there may be some ruffled feathers. Ask questions—communicate more—if you suspect unresolved issues. Often bad feelings stem from insensitivity to others: learning more about their feelings can help you improve the process for the rest of the project.

The two case studies that follow show how team members can get upset during a team-writing project. The what-went-wrong analysis for each one suggests how using the Six Steps more conscientiously can resolve or prevent such problems. This means greater productivity, too.

Case History #1: Writing audit reports—delegator assigns a solo writer

Several months ago, Linda, a specialist in DP (Data Processing) security, transferred from a supervisory position in the DP department to a staff position in the internal audit department. After her initial training, Linda was assigned to a team investigating possible unauthorized access to highly confidential corporate personnel files.

Her manager, Mr. Smith, established the customary six-week schedule for completing the report because he considered this audit a routine matter. After her initial fact gathering, Linda had trouble organizing many sections. One week before the deadline, her manager was far from pleased with Linda's draft.

Two points of view:

LINDA'S	MR. SMITH'S
I'm doing my best, but he keeps sending it back for revisions.	She has all the facts here, but they're hard to follow. Her ideas are all over the place.
If he'd just tell me what he wants, I'd be able to change it. But red ink is everywhere. He isn't explaining what I've done wrong.	I don't know where to begin editing her writing. I wish I didn't have to do her work for her.
Why should I work so hard to perfect this? The team says he'll only rewrite my material himself anyway.	We're wasting too much time on all these revisions. I might as well rewrite it myself and get it over with.

What went wrong?

1. Right from the start, there were problems with clarification and communication. Linda didn't ask enough questions. She should have asked for more direction when she felt stymied in the first place. Later, to avoid repeating her mistakes, she needed to understand why her manager corrected her work.

The manager, on the other hand, failed to offer the kind of preliminary direction to launch Linda on the project with enough information and confidence. Nor did he explain his edits so she could learn from his suggestions. Note that both members of the team shared responsibility for the communication problem; either one could have improved the situation during the process. Whenever misunderstandings develop, seldom is only one person to blame.

2. Mr. Smith found himself criticizing Linda's organization after she had invested significant time writing her first draft. If they had used the Idea Draft, Mr. Smith could have spotted and corrected Linda's Step 3 problems. Now they are faced with the painful prospect of redoing her work.

3. The manager took over too much of the Step 6 editing. Rather than trying to train Linda to produce a report appropriate for the internal audit department, Mr. Smith revised her draft for her. No wonder they were both frustrated. His detailed editing gave Linda less incentive to work on her own technique. As a last resort, he was ready to write it all himself.

Case History #2: Writing a financial management consulting proposal—delegator assigns a group of three to write

With an unusually tight deadline for a consulting proposal, Ms. Jeppson assigned her three top financial management consultants to the project. Jane and Terry had worked together before, but Tim was new to the group. Jeppson had heard he was a good writer.

When the report segments reached her the day before their deadline, she was delighted. Jane's and Terry's arrived first. It was obvious they had collaborated as usual—reviewing each other's writing before sending it to her. Tim's came in the next morning as she was rushing to leave for a meeting. Although the content was excellent in every detail, the writing style was completely different from the one that usually went out of her department. Irritated, Jeppson sent the segment back to Tim with a one-line note asking him to change his section as soon as possible to conform with the style Jane and Terry used.

Two points of view:

TIM'S	MS. JEPPSON'S
What an outrage! There's nothing wrong with this! She might at least have had the courtesy to tell me in advance that she wanted to homogenize me—like everyone else in her group.	I know how hard Tim worked, but his style just doesn't match. I hate to squelch his individuality, but anything that goes out over my signature must have a consistent style throughout. Our clients expect the best.
If that's what I get for taking the trouble to perfect my segment, I'll send in the rough draft from now on.	I'm sure that after this project, Tim will be able to submit even higher quality work.

What went wrong?

1. In a Step 6 error, the writing team didn't complete a self-review before passing the material on to the delegator. If Jane, Terry, and Tim had worked together to edit each others' segments, they would have spotted the style difference. Perhaps they could have resolved it themselves, and Tim would have had the benefit of what Jane and Terry had already learned. Jeppson should have clarified this with them in advance.

2. The manager needed to critique more supportively. All Tim heard was that his style was all wrong; he didn't realize how much Jeppson appreciated the quality of his work. As a result, she may not see that quality again. Since Tim was new, he naturally needed some orientation to standards within the group.

3. Being a good writer wasn't enough to ensure that Tim would succeed. Jeppson should have communicated her particular expectations. If she had given him a sample proposal reflecting her desired style, she could have prevented ill will and finished the proposal sooner.

In conclusion

The tips, techniques, and strategies you've read in this section will help you to be more in control of the group dynamics that affect the writing process. We don't write in a vacuum—we write *for* readers and sometimes *with* other writers. As we develop more strategic skill and political savvy, our writing becomes a tool to help us achieve our personal and professional goals. Our strategies should not be used at people's expense, but rather to win their cooperation.

PART THREE

Quiz Yourself: Find Your Personal Strengths and Weaknesses

*The great artist
is the simplifier.*
HENRI-FRÉDÉRIC AMIEL

In Step 6, we covered the critical editing skills you must apply after you've written your first draft. However, we only briefly mentioned the basic grammar skills. You must also spot and correct those errors as you follow the "Be Your Own Editor" Checklist. Although this is not a grammar book, the following quizzes should help you.

Do you need a refresher?

Most of us have a working knowledge of grammar even if we can't remember the rules. To test your grammar skills and your punctuation, try the following "Grammar: Quiz Yourself." Do the extra practice exercise if your score shows you need it. To test yourself on the editing skills we discussed in Step 6, try "Editing: Quiz Yourself," and the Practice Exercises, pages 148–155.

Grammar:
Quiz Yourself

The miniquizzes on the following pages will help you determine your strengths and weaknesses in grammar and punctuation. Each section begins with a quiz. If your score is perfect, go on to the next exercise. If you score below 100%, continue by reading the instructions and doing the practice exercise.

DANGLING MODIFIERS

Quiz Yourself

Decide whether each sentence is correct or incorrect. Check the appropriate box to the right of the sentence.

	Correct	Incorrect
1. Sounding amazingly like a human voice, she played the flute every day after work.	☐	☐
2. Lifting the heavy metal desk all alone, a vein stood out in his neck.	☐	☑
3. Although he was only an assistant vice president, the delivery boy brought him freshly brewed coffee twice a day.	☐	☐
4. While Director of Communications, several pioneering ideas became realities.	☐	☐

Answers: 1. Incorrect: Every day after work she played the flute, which sounded amazingly like a human voice. 2. Incorrect: When he lifted the heavy metal desk all alone, a vein stood out in his neck. 3. Incorrect: The delivery boy brought him freshly brewed coffee twice a day, although he was only an assistant vice-president. 4. Incorrect: Several pioneering ideas became realities while she was Director of Communications.

SCORING: 100%: Reward—go on to the quiz for parallelism. Less than 100%: Read the following guideline and complete the practice exercise.

GUIDELINE: Avoid dangling modifiers, phrases that do not logically or clearly modify a specific noun or pronoun. When you can't tell whom or what the introductory word group refers to, rearrange or add to the sentence to include the proper information. Hint: Pay special attention to the word directly after the comma. Does it belong there?

Example:

> Packed in Styrofoam, you can ship the Fogg smoke detector anywhere.

Written this way, the sentence means that *you* are packed in Styrofoam, not the detector. Here are two ways to correct this dangling modifier.

Solution #1: Add the missing subject (Fogg smoke detector) to the beginning of the main statement.

> Packed in Styrofoam, the Fogg smoke detector can be shipped anywhere.

Solution #2: Add the subject (Fogg smoke detector) and a verb to the modifying phrase to make it a clause.

> When the Fogg smoke detector is packed in Styrofoam, you can ship it anywhere.

Practice Exercise

Directions: Rewrite the sentences that contain dangling modifiers. If the sentence is correct, mark it "Correct."*

1. After spilling the soup at today's luncheon, the new Zappo contract   _____ was lost by John.

2. While I was dictating the memo, the Dictaphone fell on my toe.   _____

3. Sitting in one chair for two solid hours, the secretary's foot fell   _____ asleep.

4. By spreading the paint very thin, the painter can make one gallon   _____ cover the entire office.

5. After dictating the letter, the mailman brought the mail, which I   _____ read quickly.

*Answers are on page 157.

6. When twelve years old, her uncle was promoted to vice-president   _____
   of a multinational corporation.

7. Unless completely rewired, no engineers should handle the Zone   _____
   A electrical equipment.

8. Our curiosity was aroused, seeing a large gathering in the outer   _____
   office.

9. While circling the airport, my mind was focused on the upcoming   _____
   meeting.

10. Used for only two weeks, Jim expects to sell his home computer   _____
    for slightly less than its original cost.

PARALLELISM

Quiz Yourself

Decide whether these sentences are correct or incorrect.

	Correct	Incorrect
1. The damage was worse than they had anticipated: the rugs were stained, flood damage, and some wiring had to be replaced.	☐	☐
2. Her skills for the new job included researching, organization, and writing of long reports.	☐	☐
3. His prospective employer required five references, but his résumé contained only four, so he was worried about his chances of obtaining the job.	☐	☐
4. The personnel department couldn't decide between rental and buying a third copy machine for the upcoming rush.	☐	☐

Answers: 1. Incorrect: flood damage was extensive   2. Incorrect: organizing   3. Correct   4. Incorrect: between renting and buying

SCORING: 100%: Reward—go on to the quiz for consistency. Less than 100%: Read the guideline and complete the practice exercise.

GUIDELINE: In a sentence or a list, present parallel ideas in parallel form. In other words, sentence elements with identical functions should have identical construction. To achieve this harmony and equality of ideas, choose one form of a word, phrase, or clause and stick to it. Why? Parallel sentence elements channel the reader's attention in the same way as the refrain in a song—there's a familiar repetition to anticipate.

Example:

His typing is fast and he does it accurately.

Solution:

His typing is fast and accurate.

Practice Exercise

Directions: In the following sentences, correct the errors in parallelism. Mark "Correct" if the sentence is already correct.*

1. The agenda for the meeting is as follows:
   a. calling the meeting to order
   b. set date for next meeting
   c. taking the roll call
   d. electing new officers

2. The safety committee voted:
   a. to install lighting in the parking areas
   b. to replace handrails on the stairway
   c. that faulty electrical outlets should be replaced
   d. to improve clearing ice from the walks

3. We think she is dedicated and resourceful, and we recommend her for the job.

4. When you make the list, arrange the items in order of importance, write them in parallel form and all the items should be numbered.

5. Not only was the report disorganized and incomplete, but she misspelled many words.

6. He slept through his alarm, missed the bus, and lost his wallet, all in the same day.

7. He is efficient, thorough, and has a lot of imagination in his work.

8. By next Monday, please complete the survey, analyze the statistics, and you should hand in your report.

9. He enjoyed his new job for many reasons: the challenge, the salary, and it was a good working environment.

10. To conserve energy, follow this procedure when you leave the office:
    a. check that all electrical equipment has been turned off
    b. make sure all windows are closed
    c. are any lights left on?

*Answers are on page 158.

CONSISTENCY

Quiz Yourself

Are the following sentences correct or incorrect? Indicate your answer on the right.

	Correct	Incorrect

1. Sometimes a person gives short shrift to exercise because they don't know how to fit it into a busy schedule. ☐ ☐

2. It was the third time that she missed her bus and was late for work. Finally, she falls into her chair, exhausted before the day begins. How long could she go on this way? ☐ ☐

3. The office needed not only a long table for conferences, but also a new filing cabinet and a place to store old correspondence. ☐ ☐

4. Is it possible that television is a disruptive force in society? Do they keep us from reading books and magazines, traditionally the primary sources for obtaining information? ☐ ☐

Answers: 1. Incorrect: Sometimes a person/because he (or she) doesn't *or* Sometimes people/ because they don't. 2. Incorrect: fell/began 3. Correct. 4. Incorrect: Does it keep us

SCORING: 100%: Reward—go on to the quiz for logical comparisons. Less than 100%: Read the guideline and complete the practice exercise.

GUIDELINE: Sentences and paragraphs should be consistent in tense, in agreement of verbs with subjects, and in use of pronouns. Consistency assures a logical progression of ideas and helps the reader follow your meaning.

Examples: Here are three different types of inconsistency: tense, verb-subject, and pronoun. A correct version follows each incorrect sentence.

Incorrect:

> Today the Director of Training, Mr. Hall, will appoint several new people to the committee. On his list were Kathy, Brad, and Helen.

Correct:

> Today the Director of Training, Mr. Hall, will appoint several new people to the committee. On his list are Kathy, Brad, and Helen.

Incorrect:

> Each of the day-shift employees go out to lunch.

Correct:

> Each of the day-shift employees goes out to lunch.

Incorrect:

When someone has a cold, they should drink plenty of fluids.

Correct:

When someone has a cold, he/she should drink plenty of fluids.

Practice Exercise

Directions: Find and underline the inconsistencies in the following examples.*

1. Sometimes a person cannot decide whether they would rather have a raise or a vacation.

2. The computer is a time-saving, space-saving invention. They are not difficult to use.

3. To change this typewriter ribbon, first turn off the machine. Open the lid and release the red lever. Do not try to lift out the ribbon cartridge until you release the lever. Once the lever was released, the cartridge comes off easily.

4. Arriving late at work is a problem we all have from time to time. Sometimes we are late because family responsibilities conflict with work responsibilities, and you feel caught in the middle.

5. He ran up the steps, whirled through the revolving door, and tangles his coat in the door.

6. Routine tasks we can do almost without thinking. New tasks require greater concentration, but all tasks require attention to detail. Alternating the routine with the new provides a manner of refreshment and help ensure that our attention to detail never wavers.

7. The typewriter was developed during the nineteenth century. At first they had no shift-key mechanism and typed only capital letters.

8. On the day before her vacation, she handed in her report, answered all pending correspondence, and organizes her desk.

9. Concentration is the greater part of any skill. If a person wishes to learn a new skill, they must know how to concentrate.

10. If a reader wants to increase his reading speed, he should first learn to examine the entire book or article in question. He should learn to gather the big ideas in a selection before looking at the details. You should strive to master this technique in order to read more quickly.

*Answers are on page 158.

LOGICAL COMPARISONS

Quiz Yourself

Decide whether the following sentences are correct or incorrect and check the appropriate boxes.

	Correct	Incorrect
1. The new employee's Spanish was better than many native speakers.	☐	☐
2. He was better prepared for his speech than any other speech I've heard in a long time.	☐	☐
3. The consultant's time-management study proved that our strategy is more efficient than ITT.	☐	☐
4. This is among the easiest, if not the easiest, quiz I've ever taken.	☐	☐

Answers: 1. Incorrect: better than that of many 2. Incorrect: than any other speaker I've heard 3. Incorrect: than ITT's 4. Incorrect: among the easiest quizzes I've ever taken, if not the easiest.

SCORING: 100%: Reward—go on to the quiz for pronoun agreement. Less than 100%: Read the guidelines and complete the practice exercise.

GUIDELINE #1: When making comparisons, clearly identify the parallels or differences between the things you compare. You can make logical comparisons only between things of the same class.

GUIDELINE #2: If you want to make two comparisons in the same sentence, be sure to complete the first before starting the second.

Example:

This is one of the best products we manufacture, if not the best.

Practice Exercise

Directions: The following sentences are ambiguous as they stand. Delete, add, or rearrange words as needed to make logical comparisons.*

1. Our policies are different from Lang Realty.

2. Boston Oil's policy on absenteeism is like Acme Industries.

3. Roy is not only one of the most progressive but also dynamic leaders in our region.

4. I know the treasurer better than the general manager.

*Answers are on page 159.

5. Jim's cash outlay amounted to fifty dollars more than his partner.

6. Rob plays golf more than his friends.

7. Our health benefits are different from our competitor.

8. Sarah's sales report is better organized than her assistant.

9. My office is bigger than my boss.

PRONOUN AGREEMENT

Quiz Yourself

Are these sentences correct or incorrect? Check the appropriate box for each.

	Correct	Incorrect
1. Susan was clearer than me about her choice for president.	☐	☐
2. Between you and I, I feel that the proposal was not fair to minority groups.	☐	☐
3. Us optimists have to stick together.	☐	☐
4. If a person makes a mistake, they should admit it, and not hide the truth.	☐	☐

Answers: 1. Incorrect: clearer than I 2. Incorrect: Between you and me 3. Incorrect: We optimists 4. Incorrect: he or she should admit it

SCORING: 100%: Reward—go on to the quiz for commas. Less than 100%: Read the guidelines and complete the practice exercise.

GUIDELINE #1: If a pronoun replaces or functions as the subject of a clause or sentence, use:

Singular	Plural
I	we
you	you
he	they
she	
it	

Example:

The devil made me do it.   He made me do it.

GUIDELINE #2: If a pronoun replaces or functions as the object of a verb or preposition, use:

Singular	Plural
me	us
you	you
him	them
her	
it	

Example:

a. The memo praised Brian.   The memo praised him.
b. Send the letter to Sally and Greg.   Send the letter to her and Greg.

Remember: Before choosing a pronoun, determine how you will use it in the sentence. Also decide whether the pronoun is replacing a single or plural noun(s). Remember the guideline for consistency!

Practice Exercise

Directions: Think carefully about the function of each pronoun in the sentences below. Circle the correct form.*

Example:

Are you going to leave with (them, they) or (we, us)?

1. Between you and (I, me), the company seems on the edge of bankruptcy.
2. Two men, Dale and (he, him), made the decision.
3. (We, Us) architects must consider beauty as well as strength in our designs.
4. Mr. Skeffington showed (we, us) newcomers the training film.
5. Hal was more irritated about the bill than (I, me).
6. (She, Her) and (me, I) were the only ones who could have done the job.
7. If we need to brainstorm, I'd like to include (he, him) and Tim.
8. Among (us, we) executives at the conference, there were many from Chicago.
9. Alice and (she, her) wrote the speech.
10. The award for the best speech of the year went to Alice and (she, her).

*Answers are on page 159.

COMMAS

Quiz Yourself

Which sentences require commas? Circle the number before each sentence that needs a comma and indicate where the commas should go.

1. Steven Marx who has a melodious voice is very effective on the telephone.
2. The office that he works in is spacious.
3. Anyone who has studied computer programing has an edge in today's job market.
4. He will take advice from any person he considers knowledgeable.
5. This system which has been tested in twenty-five major office buildings across the country is infallible.

Answers: 1. Steven Marx, who has a melodious voice, is very effective on the telephone. 2. Correct 3. Correct 4. Correct 5. This system, which has been tested in twenty-five major office buildings across the country, is infallible.

SCORING: 100%: Reward—go on to the quiz for semicolons. Less than 100%: Read the guideline and complete the practice exercise.

GUIDELINE: Use commas around phrases or clauses when the information in them offers added facts about the subject.

If the phrase could be omitted because it isn't essential to the meaning of the sentence, use commas to set it off.

Example #1:

Mr. Thompson, who is in his late fifties, is the owner of the firm.

Solution #1: The clause "who is in his late fifties" is an added fact about Mr. Thompson. You could omit it and not alter the meaning of the sentence. Therefore, use commas.

Example #2:

All employees who work this Sunday will be paid overtime.

Solution #2: The clause "who work this Sunday" could not be omitted. It is essential to the meaning of the sentence because it identifies *which* employees. Therefore, do not use commas.

Directions: Supply the missing commas where needed.*

1. Our company which employs 1,800 people is the largest manufacturer in the area.
2. The men and women who work in management are well motivated.
3. People will usually try harder for a boss whom they consider fair.
4. The earth which has a limited amount of fossil-fuel resources can support only a finite number of people and their homes, cars, planes, and offices.
5. Any person who is as intelligent as Donna can have a job with the firm.
6. I have never known a manager who was as efficient as Frank.
7. Janet Brock who has never missed a day of work was promoted yesterday.
8. I believe that a firm should not manufacture any product that is useless to society.
9. This desk which was purchased in 1978 is Mr. Dooley's pride and joy.
10. Often the people who are the loudest have the least to say.

SEMICOLONS

Quiz Yourself

Are these sentences correct or incorrect?

	Correct	Incorrect
1. The department's trip to the Ice Follies was canceled; because of the bad storm and the warning of local authorities to stay off the roads.	☐	☐
2. The dog is an orphan, we found him abandoned in a cardboard box.	☐	☐
3. Our two new computers take up a lot of office space, consequently, we must now rearrange the furniture.	☐	☐
4. Working in the training department was a wise choice for Nancy; she is a natural with people.	☐	☐

Answers: 1. Incorrect (no semicolon) 2. Incorrect: orphan; we found 3. Incorrect: space; consequently, 4. Correct

SCORING: 100%: Reward—go on to the quiz for colons. Less than 100%: Read the guidelines and complete the practice exercise.

GUIDELINE #1: Use a semicolon to link two closely related complete sentences. Independent clauses must always precede and follow a semicolon.

*Answers are on page 159.

Example #1:

We cannot predict how long the study will take; we have never conducted this kind of study before.

GUIDELINE #2: Use a semicolon to precede independent clauses that begin with transition words such as *however, moreover, therefore, consequently,* or *for example.*

Example #2:

This training manual is confusing; moreover, it lacks an index and a table of contents.

GUIDELINE #3: Use a semicolon to separate items in a list or series when any item contains a comma.

Example #3:

The three people authorized to sign the check are Mr. Davis, the president; Mr. Shelby, the treasurer; and Mr. Trawler, the office manager.

Practice Exercise

Directions: Decide which sentences below require semicolons. Write the correct punctuation, the word preceding it, and any other change on the line provided.*

1. This is the warmest corner of the office it gets direct afternoon sun.   _____
2. The department needs the new equipment, however, there is no room to install it.   _____
3. We'd like everyone to contribute something to the staff party for example, bring cheese, crackers, cider, soda, cake, or cookies.   _____
4. When I'm on time, no one notices when I'm late, the whole office knows.   _____
5. The telephone survey showed that the bank's services were little known consequently, the PR department started a new publicity campaign.   _____
6. The managers had planned to discontinue that service however, an overwhelming customer demand persuaded them to retain it.   _____
7. We enjoyed our visit to the word-processing department more-over, we were glad to meet the staff.   _____
8. We are tightening security therefore, we will not issue night passes this year.   _____
9. She dislikes committee work consequently, she declined the position.   _____
10. If you need more exercise, don't use the elevator take the stairs.   _____

*Answers are on page 159.

11. We would like to give him a farewell party however, he would prefer that we do not. _____

12. We cannot meet this deadline we would like an extension. _____

13. He opened my mail for me while I was on vacation he even answered most of my letters. _____

14. The job carries several diverse responsibilities for example, you must prepare the budget, design and implement new systems, and oversee a staff of six. _____

15. We have several choices, all of them interesting. _____

16. The company softball team lost two out of three games this summer, but morale remained high. _____

COLONS

Quiz Yourself

Which of these sentences are punctuated correctly?

	Correct	Incorrect
1. Marianne is brilliant in her field: artificial intelligence.	☐	☐
2. We need to order the following; 500 letterheads, 500 envelopes, 1,000 sticky labels, and 3 reams of typing paper.	☐	☐
3. Whoever enters the room next gets this envelope: it's the door prize.	☐	☐
4. Dear Ms. Merton,	☐	☐

Answers: 1. Correct 2. Incorrect: following; 3. Correct 4. Incorrect in a business letter: Merton: (correct in a personal letter)

SCORING: 100%: Reward—go on to the quiz for dashes. Less than 100%: Read the guidelines and complete the practice exercise.

GUIDELINE #1: Use a colon after a surname in the salutation of a business letter.

Example #1:

Dear Ms. Culpepper:

GUIDELINE #2: Use a colon to link a list or series to its connecting thought.

Example #2:

Six states are participating in the conference: New Jersey, Oklahoma, New York, Florida, Texas, and California.

CAUTION: It is incorrect to use a colon after a preposition or after a form of the verb "to be."

GUIDELINE #3: Use a colon to introduce an amplification of a statement or idea. When used this way the colon replaces such words as *that is, namely,* or *for example.*

Example #3:

There is only one way to do things: the right way.

Practice Exercise

Directions: Decide where colons should replace commas. Write the new punctuation and the word preceding it in the space provided. Mark *C* if the sentence is correct as is.*

1. Make an outline, headline each paragraph, begin each paragraph _____ with a topic sentence, and proofread for spelling and punctuation.

2. Several of the smaller, more common office supplies were auto- _____ mated within the last few years, the pencil sharpener, the eraser, the stapler, the paper punch.

3. The nurse gave him the same old advice, drink plenty of liquids, _____ get lots of rest, and eat oranges.

4. We have three salesmen in each of our four regions the Northeast, _____ the mid-Atlantic states, the Northwest, the Southwest.

5. The board met in January but could not take a vote, the chair- _____ woman, the secretary, the treasurer, and two members were absent with the flu.

6. There is only one thing to dispel the midwinter gloom in this office, _____ a party.

7. Vacation time increases with length of service, one week the first _____ year, two weeks the second through the fifth year, three weeks thereafter.

8. I cannot begin without the following supplies, 40 diskettes, com- _____ puter paper, 50 overhead transparencies, a surge protector.

9. We all know why business is booming, Christmas is a week away. _____

10. Dear Fred, _____

DASHES

Quiz Yourself

Which of these sentences are punctuated correctly?

	Correct	Incorrect
1. Formal words can make you sound insecure—something no manager can afford.	☐	☐

*Answers are on page 159.

2. The book begins with the simplest writing task—a short letter or □ □
   memo—and then moves on to more challenging issues.
3. Please wait—while I run back for my briefcase. □ □
4. Her eyes kept returning to the page—the blank page. □ □

Answers: 1. Correct 2. Correct 3. Incorrect (no dash) 4. Correct

SCORING: 100%: Reward—go on to the quiz for apostrophes. Less than 100%: Read the guidelines and complete the practice exercise.

GUIDELINE #1: Use a dash to indicate an emphatic pause.

Example #1:

He knew he was in trouble—the steam gauge had exploded.

GUIDELINE #2: Use a dash to repeat an idea for emphasis.

Example #2:

The office was cold—ice-cold.

GUIDELINE #3: Use dashes to set off an explanatory expression that needs emphasis.

Example #3:

Herb brought the whole family—even the baby—to the office party.

Practice Exercise

DIRECTIONS: Decide if a dash could improve the following sentences. Some are correct either way. Write the new punctuation and the word(s) preceding and following it in the space provided.*

1. The suburban branch will be closed by the end of this month, _____
   unless its sales pick up unexpectedly.
2. He designed, produced, and distributed the posters you saw _____
   around the building.
3. Only one computer, the XR70, can perform all the functions listed _____
   here.
4. The manager was new to the firm, brand new. _____
5. If I were you, and I'm glad I'm not, I'd rewrite the report. _____
6. All our employees, clerks included, are eligible for the profit- _____
   sharing plan after two years' consecutive service.

*Answers are on page 160.

7. I gave many specific examples, all well documented. Still, no one _____
   understood the problem.
8. Please stop, I've heard all these arguments before. _____
9. If this trend continues, and there is no reason why it should not, _____
   we will show unprecedented profits this year.
10. You are the last one included in our retirement plan; you signed
    up just in time.

APOSTROPHES

Quiz Yourself

Which of these sentences are correct?

	Correct	*Incorrect*
1. When the package arrived in the mailroom, we were mystified by it's contents.	☐	☐
2. Look what she has accomplished in only two years time.	☐	☐
3. Genes happiness with the job was a pleasure to see, and his enthusiasm was contagious.	☐	☐
4. Please go to the back door; its the only one open.	☐	☐

Answers: 1. Incorrect: its 2. Incorrect: years' 3. Incorrect: Gene's 4. Incorrect: it's

SCORING: 100%: Go on to "Editing: Quiz Yourself." Less than 100%: Read the guidelines and complete the practice exercise.

GUIDELINE #1: Form the possessive of a singular noun or a plural noun not ending in *s* by adding an apostrophe and an *s*. Form the possessive of a plural noun ending in *s* by adding only the apostrophe—for example, *"a managers' meeting," "the two technicians' findings."*

GUIDELINE #2: Use the apostrophe alone, also, to form the possessive of plurals ending in *es*, as in *"the Joneses' house."*

GUIDELINE #3: Apostrophes are traditionally used in forming the plural of letters and numbers (*p*'s and *q*'s), but the more modern approach is to drop apostrophes whenever the meaning will not be affected—for example, *1930s* or *Xenon 3900s*. Always add both an apostrophe and an *s* to form the singular possessive, however (*the YMHA's building fund*).

Practice Exercise

Directions: The following sentences need apostrophes. Put the nineteen missing apostrophes in their proper places.*

1. His glasses always seem to end up on Franks desk.
2. Fridays sales meeting was canceled on account of Mr. Jones illness.
3. The new assistants job is to proofread all of the defending lawyers and the prosecuting attorneys briefs before the trials.
4. Smith & Dawsons computer is the same model as Royal Regions.
5. Jims insistence that he can't work with Mary makes the offices atmosphere tense.
6. Working womens needs are different from working mens.
7. Sudden starts and stops wear down a machines gears and sprockets.
8. The mans office is across from the womens locker room.
9. She thought Sarahs reports were more carefully researched than either Dawns or hers.
10. The XR70s cost is greater than the 3200s, which was developed in the 1980s.

*Answers are on page 160.

Editing: Quiz Yourself

The following guidelines, quizzes, and practice exercises supplement the editing skills explained in Step 6. If you need more practice, go back to Step 6 and study the related sections there.

STREAMLINED SENTENCES

Quiz Yourself

Decide whether each sentence needs streamlining. Indicate your answer at the right.

	Yes	No

1. The critical factor here is to make sure that all the machines that are heavily used are checked not fewer than two times a year. ☐ ☐

2. The information provided in this accounting seminar can only make improvements in my future accounting assignments required for the job. ☐ ☐

3. He has accomplished the development of many excellent computer programs for more than one company, which therefore seems to have given him the experience and knowledge of the skills necessary to succeed in this position. ☐ ☐

4. Our requirement is to make available the ability to prepare several versions of expense units based on probable variations. ☐ ☐

Answers: 1. Yes: It is critical to check all heavily used machines at least twice a year. 2. Yes: This accounting seminar can only improve my future on-the-job assignments. 3. Yes: He has developed many excellent computer programs for companies, so he has the experience and skill to succeed in this position. 4. Yes: We must be able to prepare several versions of expense units based on probable variations.

148

SCORING: 100%: Reward—go on to the quiz for the active voice. Less than 100%: Read the guideline and complete the practice exercise.

GUIDELINE: To prevent wordiness, ask yourself, "What is my message here?" Weed out any words or phrases that do not contribute to the reader's understanding. Use a single word to summarize a group of words; for example, *now* easily replaces *at this point in time.*

Practice Exercise

Directions: Streamline the following sentences by omitting or changing unnecessary words or phrases, rearranging sections, or dividing sentences.*

1. I certainly appreciated the chance to have the opportunity to meet with you and Arthur Forbes for lunch today, and I hope that you found our discussion to be worthwhile.

2. This letter is just a note to be sure that you and I understand what you said would be the criteria for determining the qualifications we are looking for in a new programmer for Section B.

3. What I have done is read every one of the invoices in question and pulled all the ones that I think we should have the bookkeeper look at.

4. I have a meeting scheduled with Mr. Blank on Monday to go over our fees and a few of the new requirements that some companies are asking me for.

5. Enclosed you will find various selected pages from the draft volume of the analysis guide that is being developed to help assist operators in the implementation of the new form of software.

6. As a result of a recent meeting I just had with the Personnel Department, I feel it is warranted that I recommend the hiring of Fred Brown for the position of Security Guard, which he seems well qualified for.

7. The reason for the computer blowup yesterday is really that the error file has been increasing daily, and yesterday was the day that it went over one hundred items.

8. In the unusual event that we might want to make an adjustment to the totals for any reason on the following day, we can make the needed adjustment by manually altering the figures.

9. You have asked the question as to what our fees would be.

10. Recently, I have been receiving some complaints from some nonsmoking personnel

*Streamlined sentences are on page 160.

whose most common complaint is that a nonsmoker accuses the person smoking of blowing the smoke in his direction.

11. If the stock arrives without any identification as to whom it belongs to, it can involve quite a bit of time in tracking it down.

12. I am now in the process of duplicating my draft and plan on spending some time working tonight so that my assistant may have it retyped and delivered to you by noon tomorrow.

13. If there is any further information you need, please do not hesitate to contact me.

ACTIVE VOICE

Quiz Yourself

In each pair of sentences, which is better, A or B?

	A	B
1. (A) Many important novels of American life were written by John Steinbeck. (B) John Steinbeck wrote many important novels of American life.	☐	☐
2. (A) The person on my right cleared the desk, and the person on my left swept the floor. (B) The desk was cleared by the person on my right, and the floor swept by the person on my left.	☐	☐
3. (A) You can give suggestions and comments about this memo without hurting my feelings. (B) Suggestions and comments can be given about this memo without hurting my feelings.	☐	☐
4. (A) The astronomy lecture was delivered to a large audience, and the speaker was animated and clear. (B) The speaker, who was animated and clear, delivered the astronomy lecture to a large audience.	☐	☐

Answers: 1. B; 2. A; 3. A; 4. B

SCORING: 100%: Reward—go on to the quiz for gobbledygook. Less than 100%: Read the guideline and complete the practice exercise.

GUIDELINE: Use the active voice as often as possible. If you must use the passive voice, do so only after careful consideration.

Practice Exercise

Directions: Change the following sentences from the passive to the active voice by rearranging them to show who or what is the agent—the doer of the action. Supply an agent if necessary.*

1. Her proposal ought to be given our serious consideration.
2. This conference, as was true also of the last one, was made possible through the outstanding organizing abilities of one person.
3. Confirmation is given by the data concerning the rising rate of turnover in our department.
4. All the lights should be turned off before you leave the office.
5. It is expected that our president will be told that our best client was hopelessly alienated by our new salesperson.
6. An analysis of this toxic substance will be disclosed soon.
7. It has been decided that a time clock will be installed.
8. Variable fields are indicated on the screen by underscores, so that as you enter information, the underscores are replaced by the data that you enter.
9. A decision has to be reached soon, or the contract may be lost.
10. This intolerable situation must be remedied immediately.

GOBBLEDYGOOK

Quiz Yourself

In each pair of sentences, which contains gobbledygook, A or B?

		A	B
1.	(A) The company must turn to top-priority tasks to reach its goal.	☐	☐
	(B) It is now incumbent on the company to prioritize its tasks within the parameters of its goal expectation.	☐	☐
2.	(A) Andrea's real skill performance on the job showed a negative correlation with her potential skill performance.	☐	☐
	(B) Andrea did not do as well in the job as she could have.	☐	☐
3.	(A) In answer to your letter of January 26, I am working on a solution that will be mutually satisfactory.	☐	☐
	(B) Regarding your letter of January 26, which I am now in possession of, I beg your indulgence while I frame a response that does not give preferential treatment to either your company or ours.	☐	☐
4.	(A) At the agency, the work-difficulty element involved rendered inoperative their expectation of task completion within the originally prescribed time-frame.	☐	☐

*See page 160 for corrected sentences.

(B) The agency's work was so difficult that the employees did not   ☐   ☐
finish on time.

Answers: 1. B; 2. A; 3. B; 4. A

SCORING: 100%: Reward—go on to the quiz on words and tone. Less than 100%: Read the guideline and complete the practice exercise.

GUIDELINE: To avoid gobbledygook, use the simplest, most concise language that will accurately express your ideas.

Practice Exercise

Directions: Rewrite the following sentences to eliminate gobbledygook.*

1. The termination of the product line will facilitate the advancement of the company's overall sales.

2. We would like to ask that you forward your spouse's Social Security number to the firm at your earliest convenience.

3. In view of the fact that the treasurer deems it important to institute a policy terminating managers over age sixty-eight, we will peruse his recommendations most seriously.

4. During the course of the week, Mr. Jones has utilized every available source to locate the materials.

5. We are in need of your assistance in ascertaining what has transpired since we first communicated.

6. Your cooperation in obtaining information as to the residences of employees hired prior to 1986 would be appreciated.

7. Did you obtain a copy of Mr. Quibble's communication requesting all personnel to indicate in writing when they intend to make use of a company vehicle?

8. I am contacting you with respect to initiating a stress-management program within the confines of our office building.

9. Did you sustain any mental or physical injuries as a consequence of the accident?

10. We would like to request that you comply with the ensuing directions and complete the attached forms in detail.

*Suggested answers are on page 161.

WORDS AND TONE

Quiz Yourself

Choose another word—a less formal one—for each of the blank spaces below.

1. sufficient _____
2. to supply _____
3. to incorporate _____
4. to transpire _____

SCORING: 100%: Reward—go on to the quiz for positive approach. Less than 100%: Read the guideline and complete the practice exercise.

GUIDELINE: Don't use an inflated word if a down-to-earth one will do the job as well.

Practice Exercise

Directions: Fill in each blank using a less formal word with the same meaning.*

1. to anticipate _____
2. to apprise _____
3. to ascertain _____
4. to assist _____
5. to concur _____
6. to deem _____
7. to desire _____
8. to determine _____
9. to disclose _____
10. to effect _____
11. to endeavor _____
12. to ensue _____
13. to execute _____
14. to forward _____
15. to furnish _____
16. inasmuch as _____
17. to indicate _____
18. initially _____
19. in lieu of _____
20. in the event that _____
21. to locate _____
22. to state _____
23. pertaining to _____
24. presently _____
25. prior to _____
26. to prohibit _____
27. to request _____
28. to require _____
29. residence _____
30. to surmise _____

POSITIVE APPROACH

Quiz Yourself

Rewrite these sentences in a more positive way.

1. This letter isn't up to our standards.

*Suggested answers are on page 161.

2. If you don't improve your attendance record, you won't be promoted.

3. Without careful preparation, we won't be able to win the account.

4. It would not be objectionable if you attended the workshop in the fall.

SCORING: 100%: Reward—go on to "Your Personal Profile Graph." Less than 100%: Read the guideline and complete the practice exercise.

GUIDELINE: Choose words that convey a confident, positive attitude. Avoid unnecessary negatives.

Practice Exercise

Directions: Rewrite the following sentences in a more positive way.*

1. We hope you will not be disappointed with the results.

2. Without proper planning, we will not be able to prevent overcrowding.

3. We are sorry, but we cannot process your order until you have paid the balance on your account.

4. If you don't like my suggestions, please contact me.

5. No doubt the changes should prove worthwhile.

6. Do not ignore details; they are important.

7. This job is going to be nearly impossible to do.

YOUR PERSONAL PROFILE GRAPH

Now that you've polished your skills, start applying what you've learned to your daily writing. Editing will be easier if you have a list of your strengths and weaknesses before you. This will remind you to apply actively what you've learned. Use the graph on page 155 to map your skills. Then make a list of your weaknesses and post it by your desk for quick reference when editing.

*Suggested answers are on page 161.

How to Fill Out the Graph: Flip back through the practice exercises in Part Three and note your strengths and weaknesses in each by calculating your percentage of correct answers. Consider a score of less than 70% a weakness. To complete the profile, plot your scores on the graph shown below. You might also want to post a copy of the graph next to your list of weaknesses.

Personal Profile Graph

Score—% Correct

	10%	20%	30%	40%	50%	60%	70%	80%	90%	100%
Dangling Modifiers										
Parallelism										
Consistency										
Logical Comparisons										
Pronoun Agreement										
Commas										
Semicolons										
Colons										
Dashes										
Apostrophes										
Streamlined Sentences										
Active Voice										
Gobbledygook										
Words and Tone										
Positive Agreement										

Editing: Quiz Yourself

You've finished this book. You've applied the Six Steps. It's time for you to develop your own plan for putting your new skills into action.

DIRECTIONS: Make a list of your intentions for your next writing project. What will you do differently? What are your writing goals?

MY ACTION PLAN

APPENDIX A
Solutions to Exercises

MARKETING LETTERS RESPONSE SHEET *(from page 91)*

1. The second one.
2. Pompous, insulting, condescending, cold.
3. Friendly, warm, sincere, down-to-earth, the "you" attitude.
4. Her own company.
5. The interests and needs of the potential client, Dewitt.
6. #2. It was lively and competent. Goodman sounded like a go-getter.
7. #2. She suggests an exact date. Good idea!

DANGLING MODIFIERS *(from page 132)*

1. After spilling the soup at today's luncheon, John lost the new Zappo contract.
2. Correct
3. The secretary's foot fell asleep after she sat in one chair for two solid hours.
4. Correct
5. The mailman brought the mail, which I read quickly after dictating the letter.
6. Her uncle was promoted to vice-president of a multinational corporation when she was twelve years old.
7. Unless the Zone A electrical equipment is completely rewired, no engineer should handle it.
8. Our curiosity was aroused after we saw a large gathering in the outer office.
9. While we circled the airport, my mind was focused on the upcoming meeting.
10. Jim expects to sell his home computer, used for only two weeks, for slightly less than its original cost.

PARALLELISM   *(from page 134)*

There are two possible solutions to #1.

1. a. Correct   or: a. call the meeting to order
   b. setting the date for the next meeting   b. set the date for the next meeting
   c. Correct   c. take the roll call
   d. Correct   d. elect new officers
2. a. Correct
   b. Correct
   c. to replace faulty electrical outlets
   d. Correct
3. Correct
4. When you make the list, arrange the items in order of importance, write them in parallel form, and number them.
5. Her report was not only disorganized and incomplete, but it was also full of misspelled words.
6. Correct
7. He is efficient, thorough, and imaginative in his work.
8. By next Monday, please complete the survey, analyze the statistics, and hand in your report.
9. He enjoyed his new job for many reasons: the challenge, the salary, and the working environment.
10. a. Correct
    b. Correct
    c. make sure no lights are left on

CONSISTENCY   *(from page 136)*

1. Sometimes people cannot decide whether they would rather have a raise or a vacation. *or* Sometimes a person cannot decide whether he (*or* she) would rather have a raise or a vacation.
2. It is not difficult to use.
3. Once you release the lever, the cartridge comes off easily.
4. Sometimes we are late because family responsibilities conflict with work responsibilities and we feel caught in the middle.
5. He ran up the steps, whirled through the revolving door, and tangled his coat in the door.
6. Alternating the routine with the new provides a manner of refreshment and helps ensure that our attention to detail never wavers.
7. At first it had no shift-key mechanism and typed only capital letters.
8. On the day before her vacation, she handed in her report, answered all pending correspondence, and organized her desk.
9. If a person wishes to learn a new skill, he (*or* she) must know how to concentrate.
10. He should strive to master this technique in order to read more quickly.

LOGICAL COMPARISONS *(from page 137)*

1. Our policies are different from Lang Realty's (policy's).
2. Boston Oil's policy on absenteeism is like Acme Industry's (policy).
3. Roy is not only one of the most progressive leaders in our region, he's also the most dynamic.
4. I know the treasurer better than I know the general manager.
5. Jim's cash outlay amounted to fifty dollars more than his partner's (cash outlay).
6. Rob plays golf more than his friends do.
7. Our health benefits are different from our competitor's (health benefits).
8. Sarah's sales report is better organized than her assistant's.
9. My office is bigger than my boss's (office).

PRONOUN AGREEMENT *(from page 139)*

1. me 2. he 3. We 4. us 5. I 6. She, I 7. him 8. us 9. she 10. her

COMMAS *(from page 141)*

1. Our company, which employs 1,800 people, is the largest manufacturer in the area.
2. Correct
3. Correct
4. The earth, which has a limited amount of fossil-fuel resources, can support only a finite number of people and their homes, cars, planes, and offices.
5. Correct
6. Correct
7. Janet Brock, who has never missed a day of work, was promoted yesterday.
8. Correct
9. This desk, which was purchased in 1978, is Mr. Dooley's pride and joy.
10. Correct

SEMICOLONS *(from page 142)*

1. office;
2. equipment;
3. party;
4. notices;
5. known;
6. service;
7. department;
8. security;
9. work;
10. elevator;
11. party;
12. deadline;
13. vacation;
14. responsibilities;
15. Correct
16. Correct

COLONS *(from page 144)*

1. Correct 2. years:* 3. advice:* 4. regions: 5. vote:† 6. office:* 7. service:
8. supplies: 9. booming: 10. Correct

*A colon is not the only acceptable solution here. See the section on dashes.
†A semicolon, instead of a colon, is also correct.

DASHES *(from page 145)*

1. month—unless
2. Correct
3. computer—the XR70—can
4. firm—brand new
5. you—and I'm glad I'm not—I'd
6. employees—clerks included—are
7. examples—all
8. stop—I've
9. continues—and there is no reason why it should not—we
10. plan—you

APOSTROPHES *(from page 147)*

1. Frank's
2. Friday's, Jones's
3. assistant's, lawyers', attorneys'
4. Dawson's, Region's
5. Jim's, office's
6. women's, men's
7. machine's
8. man's, women's
9. Sarah's, Dawn's
10. XR70's, 3200's; either 1980s or 1980's is correct

STREAMLINED SENTENCES *(from page 149)*

There are many correct solutions to these. Here are mine:

1. I was pleased to have lunch with you and Arthur Forbes today. I hope you found our discussion worthwhile.
2. I want to confirm our criteria for determining the qualifications of a new Section B programmer.
3. I have pulled all the invoices I feel the bookkeeper should review.
4. On Monday, Mr. Blank and I will meet to discuss our fees and some new company requirements.
5. Enclosed are some pages from the draft of the analysis guide we're developing to help operators implement the new software.
6. After meeting with the Personnel Department, I recommend Fred Brown for the Security Guard position—he is well qualified.
7. The computer blew up yesterday because the error file went over one hundred items.
8. If we want to adjust the totals on the following day, we can do so manually.
9. You asked about our fees.
10. Recently, nonsmokers have complained that smokers are blowing smoke in their direction.
11. Tracking down unidentified stock can be time-consuming.
12. I'll work on my draft tonight so that you'll have it tomorrow.
13. If you need more information, please contact me.

ACTIVE VOICE *(from page 151)*

1. We should give her proposal our serious consideration.
2. One person's outstanding organizing abilities made the conference possible both this year and last.
3. The data confirm the rising turnover rate in our department.
4. Please turn off all lights before you leave the office.

5. We expect someone to tell our president that our new salesperson hopelessly alienated our best client.
6. We will soon disclose an analysis of this toxic substance.
7. Management has decided to install a time clock.
8. The information you enter replaces the underscores that indicate variable fields on the screen.
9. We must reach a decision soon, or we may lose the contract.
10. We must remedy this intolerable situation immediately.

GOBBLEDYGOOK   *(from page 152)*

1. Dropping this product line will improve the company's overall sales.
2. Please send the firm your spouse's Social Security number as soon as possible.
3. Because the treasurer feels it is important to start letting go managers over age sixty-eight, we will read his recommendation seriously.
4. This week, Mr. Jones asked everybody he knew to help him find the materials.
5. We need your help in order to find out what happened since we first telephoned you.
6. Would you please help us find the home addresses of employees hired before 1986?
7. Did you get a copy of Mr. Quibble's memo asking all employees to inform him in writing when they need a company car?
8. Would you be interested in starting a stress-management program in our office building?
9. Were you injured in the accident?
10. Kindly follow the directions and complete the attached forms in detail.

WORDS AND TONE   *(from page 153)*

1. to expect	11. to try	21. to find
2. to tell	12. to follow	22. to say
3. to find out	13. to do	23. of or about
4. to help	14. to send	24. soon
5. to agree with	15. to give	25. before
6. to consider or think	16. since	26. to forbid or prevent
7. to want	17. to say or show	27. to ask for
8. to find out	18. at first	28. to need
9. to tell	19. instead of	29. home or address
10. to cause or bring about	20. if	30. to guess

POSITIVE APPROACH   *(from page 154)*

1. We're sure you will be pleased with the results.
2. With proper planning, there will be space for everyone.
3. As soon as we receive your payment, we will process your order.
4. If you want to comment on my suggestions, please contact me.
5. We expect the changes to be beneficial.
6. Pay attention to details; they are important.
7. This job is going to be a challenge.

APPENDIX B
The Spelling Cheat Sheet

THE SPELLING CHEAT SHEET

If you're a bad speller, you probably hate using the dictionary, too. Who has the time? This spelling cheat sheet contains some of the words most commonly misspelled in business. Photocopy it or cut it out and keep it in your desk drawer. Highlight the words that you miss most frequently.

An audit of spelling ability would show that each of us has a personal list of hard-to-spell words that are our special bugaboos. If you're stuck for a word that's not on the Cheat Sheet, find it in the dictionary and add it to the sheet. Pinpoint your errors once and for all so that they'll be just a glance away.

abbreviate	accordance	admirable	allotment
abruptly	accrued	advantageous	allotted
absence	accumulate	advertisement	allowable
absolutely	accuracy	advertising	allowance
accede	achievement	advice	all right
acceleration	acknowledgment	advisable	almost
accept	acquaintance	advise	already
acceptance	acquiesce	adviser	although
accessible	acquire	advisory	altogether
accessory	address	affect	ambitious
accidentally	adequate	affidavit	amendment
accommodate	adjourn	aggravate	analysis
accompanying	adjustment	agreeable	analyze

announce
announcement
annoyance
annual
anticipate
apologize
apparent
appearance
applicable
applicant
appointment
appraisal
appreciable
appropriate
approximate
architect
argument
arrangement
article
ascertain
assessment
assignment
assistance
associate
assured
attendance
attorneys
authorize
available

bankruptcy
bargain
basis
believable
believe
beneficial
beneficiary
benefited
biennially
bookkeeper
brilliant
brochure

budget
bulletin
bureau
business

calendar
canceled
cancellation
candidate
capital
capitol
casualty
catalog
cease
ceiling
choice
choose
circumstances
client
clientele
collateral
column
commission
commitment
committee
comparable
compelled
competent
competitor
complement
compliment
compromise
concede
conceivable
conceive
concession
concurred
conference
confident
confidential
congratulate
conscience

conscientious
conscious
consensus
consequence
consignment
consistent
conspicuous
continual
continuous
controlling
controversy
convenience
convenient
cordially
correspondence
council
counsel
courteous
courtesy
creditor
criticism
criticize
current
customer

debtor
deceive
decision
deductible
defendant
defense
deferred
deficit
definite
definitely
delegate
dependent
depositors
describe
desirable
deteriorate
develop

development
device
devise
differed
difference
director
disappear
disappoint
discrepancy
dissatisfied
division
dual

eagerly
economical
effect
efficiency
efficient
either
eligible
eliminate
eminent
emphasis
emphasize
employee
endeavor
endorsement
enterprise
enthusiasm
envelop
envelope
environment
equipment
equipped
equivalent
especially
essential
etiquette
evident
exaggerate
exceed
excellence

excellent
except
excessive
exclusively
exercise
existence
expedite
expenditure
expense
experience
explanation
extension
extraordinary

facilities
familiarize
fascinate
favorable
favorite
feasible
February
financial
forcible
foreign
foreword
forfeit
formerly
forty
forward
fourth
freight
friend
fulfillment
furthermore

gauge
genuine
governor
grateful
grievance
guarantee

handled
harass
hardware
hazardous
height
hesitant
hindrance

identical
illegible
immediately
imminent
imperative
implement
inasmuch as
incidentally
inconvenience
incurred
indebtedness
independent
indispensable
individual
inducement
inference
inferred
influential
inquiry
installment
intelligence
intention
intercede
intercession
interfere
interrupted
inventory
investor
irregular
irrelevant
itemized
itinerary
it's, its

jeopardize
judgment
justifiable

knowledge

laboratory
legible
legitimate
leisure
letterhead
liaison
library
license
likable
likelihood
livelihood
loose
lose
luncheon

magazine
maintenance
management
manufacturer
manuscript
maximum
memorandum
merchandise
mileage
millennium
minimum
minuscule
mischievous
miscellaneous
modernize
mortgage

necessary
negligible
negotiate
neighborhood

neither
nevertheless
ninety
noticeable
nuisance

oblige
occasion
occupant
occurred
occurrence
occurring
offense
offering
official
omission
opportunity
optional
ordinary
organization
organize
original
overdue

pamphlet
parallel
partial
participant
particularly
patronage
perceive
percent
performance
permanent
permissible
permitted
perseverance
personal
personnel
persuade
planning
pleasant

pleasure
practical
practically
practice
precede
precision
preferable
preference
preferred
prejudice
preliminary
premium
previous
principal
principle
privilege
procedure
proceed
professor
prominent
prosecute
psychology
purchase
pursue

quantity
questionnaire
quiet
quite

realize
reasonable
receipt

receive
recently
recognize
recommend
recurrence
reference
referred
referring
regrettable
reimburse
remittance
renewal
repetition
representative
requirement
respectfully
respectively
responsibility
responsible
restaurant
ridiculous
route

salable
salary
satisfactorily
satisfying
schedule
secretary
securities
seized
separate
serviceable

several
severely
shipment
siege
significant
similar
simultaneous
sincerity
somewhat
specialize
specialty
stationary
stationery
statistics
strictly
submitted
subscriber
substantial
succeed
successful
sufficient
superintendent
supersede
supervisor
supposedly
survey

tariff
temporary
their
there
thorough
throughout

tragedy
transferred
typing

ultimately
unanimous
undoubtedly
unfortunately
unnecessary
unusually
until
usually

vacillate
vacuum
valuable
various
vehicle
vendor
vicinity
visible
voluntary
volunteer

warehouse
weather
weird
whether
wholly
withhold
worthwhile
writing

yield

Fry's Readability Graph

FRY'S READABILITY GRAPH

If you don't have a computer program for rating the readability level of your writing, you can assess it manually. (See page 99 for suggested programs.) Edward Fry, Ph.D., director of the Reading Center at Rutgers University, designed the following "Graph for Estimating Readability" of documents:

Check sentence length and word length

1. Select a 100-word passage

Word is defined as a group of symbols with a space on either side. Therefore, *Joe, JRA, 1945,* and *&* are counted as words.

2. Count the number of sentences

Round to the nearest tenth. You may have 7.6 or 8.2 sentences when you consider the fraction of the last sentence that isn't finished within the 100-word sample.

3. Count the number of syllables

Syllables are defined phonetically: there are as many syllables as vowel sounds. For example, *stopped* is one syllable and *wanted* is two syllables.

   If each word contained one syllable, you would have 100 syllables. So, you can use 100 as a base and count only the syllables in words that have more than one syllable. Tally the figures by noting these slash marks: one slash for a two-syllable word, two slashes for a three-syllable word, etc. Then, count the slashes and add that to 100.

4. Plot your results

Find your sentence total on the vertical axis of the graph below, and your syllable total on the horizontal axis. Plot a dot where the two lines intersect, and you'll see your document's readability level.

Calculate readability for several 100-word samples

Readability measurements are always rough approximations. It's an inexact method, so measuring one sample will not be enough. Plot the results of at least three samples, then estimate your readability level by averaging the three. When textbook editors rate a book, they assess samples from several chapters before arriving at a readability level.

GRAPH FOR ESTIMATING READABILITY

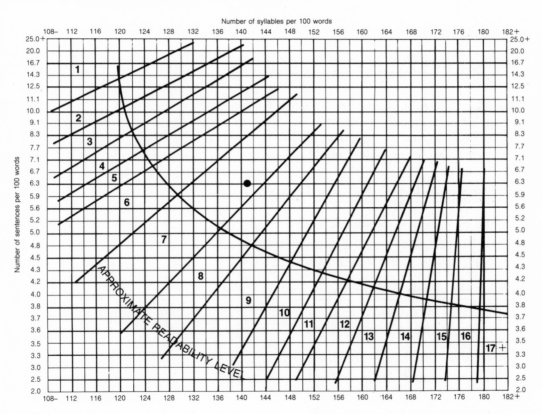

The point on the graph above represents a seventh-level sample containing 141 syllables and 6.3 sentences.

Suggested Reading

Barnet, Sylvan, and Marcia Stubbs. *Barnet & Stubbs's Practical Guide to Writing.* Boston: Little, Brown & Company, 1975.

*Blumenthal, Joseph C. *English 3200,* 3d ed. New York: Harcourt Brace Jovanovich, 1981.

*Brusaw, Charles T., Gerald J. Alred, and Walter E. Oliu. *The Business Writer's Handbook.* New York: St. Martin's Press, 1977.

Buzan, Tony. *Use Your Head.* London: British Broadcasting Corporation, 1974.

Elbow, Peter. *Writing with Power.* New York: Oxford University Press, 1981.

*Ewing, David. *Writing for Results.* New York: John Wiley & Sons, 1974.

Holcombe, Marya W., and Judith K. Stein. *Writing for Decision Makers.* Belmont, Calif.: Wadsworth Publishing Co., 1981.

Laird, Dugan. *Writing for Results.* Reading, Mass.: Addison-Wesley Publishing Co., 1978.

Miller, Casey, and Kate Swift. *The Handbook of Nonsexist Writing.* New York: Harper & Row, 1980.

Roman, Kenneth, and Joel Raphaelson. *Writing That Works.* New York: Harper & Row, 1981.

Shaw, Fran Weber. *30 Ways to Help You Write.* New York: Bantam Books, 1980.

Tichy, H. J. *Effective Writing for Engineers, Managers, Scientists.* New York: John Wiley & Sons, 1966.

Zinsser, William. *On Writing Well,* 3rd ed. New York: Harper & Row, 1985.

Zinsser, William. *Writing with a Word Processor.* New York: Harper & Row, 1983.

*Especially recommended because they contain excellent practice drills and exercises in addition to information.

ABOUT THE AUTHOR

In 1978, DEBORAH DUMAINE founded Better Communications, a firm that specializes in business, technical, sales, and audit writing workshops. A pioneer in diagnostic writing-training, Ms. Dumaine and her firm have worked with major corporations throughout the country. Better Communications is based in Boston and Los Angeles. Ms. Dumaine received her graduate and undergraduate degrees from Smith College and also did postgraduate work at the University of Iowa. She lives in Cambridge, Massachusetts.